Aldus Manutius

IVNII IVVENALIS AQVINA
TIS SATYRA PRIMA.

SEMPER EGO AVDITOR
tantum? nunquám ne reponam
V exatus toties rauci thefeide
Codri?
I mpune ergo mihi recitauerit ille
togatas?
H ic elegos? impune diem consumpserit ingens
T elephus? aut summi plena iam margine libri
S criptus, et in tergo nec dum finitus, Orestes?
N ota magis nulli domus est sua, quam mihi lucus
M artis, et æoliis uicinum rupibus antrum
V ulcani. Quid agant uenti, quas torqueat umbras
A eacus, unde alius furtiuæ deuehat aurum
P elliculæ, quantas iaculetur Monychus ornos,
F rontonis platani, conuulsáq; marmora clamant
S emper, et assiduo ruptæ lectore columnæ.
E xpectes eadem a summo, minimóq; poeta.
E t nos ergo manum ferulæ subduximus, et nos
C onsilium dedimus Syllæ, priuatus ut altum
D ormiret. stulta est clementia, cum tot ubique
V atibus occurras, perituræ parcere chartæ.
C ur tamen hoc libeat potius decurrere campo,
P er quem magnus equos Auruncæ flexit alumnus,
S i uacat, et placidi rationem admittitis, edam.
C um tener uxorem ducat spado, Meuia thuscum
F igat aprum, et nuda teneat uenabula mamma,
P atricios omnes opibus cum prouocet unus,

The Aldine Juvenal and Persius of 1501:
a copy printed on vellum and illuminated for the Pisani family of Venice.
Original page-size 166×101 mm. C.4.g.10, sig. a2.

Aldus Manutius

Printer and Publisher of Renaissance Venice

*

Martin Davies

Arizona Center for Medieval and Renaissance Studies
Tempe, Arizona
1999

First published 1995
by The British Library
Great Russell Street
London WC1B 3DG

Second Printing

Published in North America
by The Arizona Center for
Medieval and Renaissance
Studies as Volume 214 in the
series Medieval & Renaissance
Texts & Studies

NOTE
Unless otherwise specified,
pressmarks of the books illustrated
are of copies in The British Library

ALDUS MANUTIUS

*

AS WITH MOST PRINTERS OF THE FIFTEENTH CENTURY from Gutenberg onwards, we know next to nothing of Aldus Manutius before he took up, in his forties, the activity which was to give him lasting renown. He was a reticent man who seldom wrote about himself, as opposed to his work, and no early biography supplies the gaps. It is the books themselves that have to speak, with support from the occasional document or passage of humanist correspondence. He was born at Bassiano in the papal states, probably about 1451. Bassiano is a hill town some thirty-five miles south-east of Rome which would have remained unknown to fame had Aldus not styled himself 'Bassianas' in a few of his earliest books, a style soon replaced by 'Aldus Romanus'. From scattered comments here and there in the prefaces it emerges that he received some humanistic schooling at Rome, and some form of higher education at Ferrara.

It was in Rome that his life received the direction it was to take before he turned to printing. If he had been asked at any point of the 1470s or '80s what his ambition was, he might well have answered with his admired friend Politian that he wanted to be a 'grammaticus'. A good 'grammarian' (a scholar or philologist, we should say) was concerned above all to absorb, understand and expound the values of classical antiquity through the concrete vehicle of the texts which had reached the Renaissance. His master at Rome seems to have been Gaspare da Verona, a middling sort of humanist who composed a reasonably successful grammar, as well as a life of the reigning pope, Paul II, which has the distinction of being the first work to mention, under the date 1466 - 67, the advent of printing in Italy. But Aldus, we gather from a passing later reference, also had the benefit of hearing lectures at the university from one of the brightest academic stars of the day, another Veronese humanist named Domizio Calderini. It may have been Calderini that stirred in him a love of Greek, for it was Calderini's belief – one that was becoming increasingly general in Italy in the second half of the fifteenth century – that a full understanding of the Latin classics, and of the ancient world as a whole, depended on a knowledge of the Greek literature that lay behind them.

The interdependence of Greek and Latin was also prominent in the teaching

of Battista Guarino, a famous teacher at the University of Ferrara and inheritor of the chair of eloquence there from his more famous father Guarino da Verona. Whether or not he had picked up any Greek in Rome, Aldus certainly followed Battista's lessons at Ferrara, doubtless in the period 1475-80, and these included Greek literature besides courses on Latin authors. This much is known from the dedication to his old teacher of the 1496 Hesiod and Theocritus By that stage he will have been fluent in both the ancient languages, and like many another humanities graduate since, the question then arose as to how to apply his talents Schoolmastering offered itself, as it always has, and in 1480 – the first definite date of his life – we find him named as tutor to the young princes of Carpi, Alberto and Lionello Pio. The same document extended to Aldus citizenship of this small, precariously independent city just north of Modena, midway between Bologna and Mantua He seems to have spent the next few years alternating between Carpi and Ferrara, perhaps teaching in both places

Alberto, the elder of the two sons of the widowed Caterina Pio, was to be an important figure in Aldus's later career. The immediate benefit to him, however, apart from more or less steady employment, was entry into the world of their uncle, the philosopher prince of Mirandola, Giovanni Pico. He may have already become acquainted with Pico as a fellow student at Ferrara and is known to have taken refuge with him at Mirandola when Venetian armies threatened that city in 1482. Pico was a Renaissance intellectual *par excellence*, thoroughly versed in the classics, and even acquainted – a rare accomplishment – with oriental languages He had a powerful synthetic mind which attempted to harmonize Platonism, Aristotelianism and Christianity, incorporating elements of Hebrew and Arabic thought More importantly for Aldus, he was widely known and liked in the scholarly circles of Florence and Venice It is from this period, the mid-1480s, that Aldus's acquaintance with Pico's friends and fellow scholars, Ermolao Barbaro in Venice and Angelo Poliziano in Florence, probably date. Relations with Politian (as he is naturalized in English) may never have been close but they were certainly cordial, and it was later to fall to Aldus to make the first collected edition of the master's works With Barbaro, on the other hand, Politian's twin spirit at Venice, there is every reason to think that his influence was decisive on the path that Aldus took at the end of the 1480s

VENICE AND PRINTING

That path was to Venice. There is no way of telling exactly when Aldus conceived his great plan of publishing wholesale the works of ancient Greece in the original language But it is certain that the intellectual atmosphere and

In the decade 1470 to 1480 the names of some fifty printers at Venice are known, plus half a dozen anonymous firms identified only by their printing types. Unrestrained competition drove many of them out of business, particularly in a disastrous period of over-production in 1472-73. It was partly a matter of poor estimation of what sort of texts, in what numbers, the market could bear As with the earliest printing in Rome and Paris, the first Venetian printers tended to concentrate on books of classical, patristic and humanistic interest, printed in the fine roman types derived from humanist handwriting. After the crisis of 1473, a gradual change to safer texts is observable, ones for which the clergy and universities would always have a steady demand – law, scholastic philosophy, theology, from the late 1470s an increasing number of liturgies There was also a general move towards the gothic types which the conservative professions favoured. These are only tendencies. Classical authors never ceased to be printed at Venice, but not with the exclusive preoccupation of the earliest period As for typefaces, it should be be remembered that the most famous and elegant roman types of the 1470s, those of the Frenchman Nicholas Jenson, were far outnumbered by his gothic founts, which he employed a good deal more frequently in the course of his ten-year career.

Hand in hand with these developments went a consolidation of the trade into large syndicates Printing books was a capital-intensive business, speculative in its market and slow in its returns long credit and powerful backers were required to assemble the texts, types and (the most expensive item) paper needed to make an edition The two large syndicates of the 1470s – one French, based on Jenson's company, and the other German deriving from John of Speyer's original firm – joined together at the end of the decade to form a short-lived *Grande Compagnia*. These syndicates and others like them (after the death of Jenson in 1480, increasingly Italian) were very powerful organizations, with a clear differentiation of functions as between the different partners The earliest printers had secured funds, and printed, marketed and sold their books as a unified enterprise. From the mid-1470s the partners to a contract took on more and more the specialized roles of merchant backers, printers, publishers, distributors and booksellers, often with some degree of overlap. The efficient capitalist structures of the biggest firms and the constant competition both tended to drive down prices, so that for the first time in history books were widely and cheaply available throughout Europe.

The international outlook of Venetian printers and the favourable situation and traditions of the city encouraged mass export of the products of the presses from the outset. The books would travel in unbound quires, by sea to western Europe and other parts of Italy, but more especially by the land route to the large markets of southern Germany. So it came about that many Venetian

books scarcely touched on *terra firma* before passing over the Brenner to the rich Bavarian monasteries. By the 1480s the larger printers had sufficient grasp of their markets to be able to concentrate on certain types of publication with a reasonable expectation of matching supply to demand. Any diocese of Europe – even in England – which needed a new breviary for uniformity of divine service could turn to one of half a dozen Venetian specialists and be assured of a high-quality product, with good press-work and correctly registered red and black printing. Baptista de Tortis and the brothers de Gregoriis specialized in the classics in the 1480s; in the 1490s de Tortis so far controlled the trade in legal printing that a law book came to be known simply as a 'liber de Tortis'.

THE PRINTING OF GREEK

By the time Aldus arrived at the end of the 1480s Venice had attained a position of unassailable dominance in the printing of Latin books, more particularly in the profitable field of academic and liturgical texts. The situation with Greek books could not have been more different. Very little Greek printing had been done at that stage anywhere in Italy, and none at all elsewhere in Europe. For all its large Greek community, Venice lagged behind Florence and Milan in this respect. In those cities local humanist interest and émigré Byzantine scholarship had combined to have printed a small number of literary texts – including the famous Florentine Homer of 1488 – as well as the rudimentary grammars which were the staple of early Greek printing everywhere. Even little Vicenza, one of Venice's own subject towns, could show seven of these educational texts, to be set against the two solitary editions (a Greek psalter, preceded by the pseudo-Homeric mock epic *Batrachomyomachia*) that a short-lived Cretan press put out at Venice in 1486.

The reasons why something did not happen are seldom discoverable, but certain obvious points can be made. The first is that overall demand for Greek texts was very slight; what there was tended to emphasize elementary works – primers, readers and dictionaries – which could assist western Europeans to learn the language. The base of Greek learning among the Italians, though in pockets profound, was not large or widely spread. The Greeks themselves were seldom possessed of the means or the patrons to set up presses to print their own literature: the Venetian firm of Laonicus and Alexander, which produced the two editions mentioned above, was an exception, but the failure of their venture speaks for itself. The Greek people, as subjects of Venetian Crete or victims of the diaspora consequent upon the Turkish conquest of their land, did not in any case constitute a stable and concentrated market.

To these disincentives was added the greatest difficulty, that of a satisfactory

transfer of Greek script into type Greek handwriting had never undergone the various stages of reform and standardization that had allowed Latin script to be transformed into the chaste formality of Venetian gothic and roman founts. The written language was beset by ligatures and contractions in wild profusion, and the superstructure of accents and breathings that had inhered in the language since Hellenistic times made any typographical rendering technically as well as aesthetically difficult Robert Proctor at the beginning of this century calculated that the number of sorts in the fount of Laonicus and Alexander – the separate pieces of type which represented all possible forms and combinations of letters, breathings and accents – came to something over 1300 Though admittedly the most extreme case, this was not the sort of printing calculated to appeal to the hard-nosed men who ran the Venetian industry. Those Latins who were persuaded of the message of Battista Guarino and Ermolao Barbaro were generally of a sort well able to afford to have the texts they required copied out by hand The many Greek scribes in Venice, often men of great learning if also in straitened circumstances, could supply those needs. All in all the total of sixty fifteenth-century editions in Greek, including bilingual readers, begins to look less surprising Of the major Greek authors only Homer, Theocritus and part of Hesiod had reached print before the Aldine press was set up. But if Greek was a technical problem, it was also a prestigious opportunity, awaiting energy and capital.

This, then, was the situation that Aldus found when he repaired to Venice at some point towards the end of the 1480s, an unknown grammar master approaching forty. Of his contacts at this time we have only fugitive hints and equivocal inferences drawn from humanist correspondence. A letter of 1484 survives from Aldus to Politian offering friendship, in the manner of the time, and admiration of a Greek letter of Politian. This, he said, he had read in the company of the Greek scribe Emanuel Adramyttenus when they were together at Mirandola under Pico's protection in 1482. Politian's reply expresses the hope that one day they will meet to cement the friendship, here gracefully reciprocated. Aldus certainly encountered Politian in 1491 – the latter made a note of the meeting – when the Florentine was in Venice with Pico in search of books and libraries for Lorenzo de' Medici, there to be entertained by Barbaro and others. That is the limit of their known relations Four years later, in the preface to the first volume of the Greek Aristotle, Aldus had occasion to lament the death of all three of these great scholars, 'men who could rival antiquity'.

The Greek scholar and teacher Janus Lascaris had taken the same route in 1490, visiting the libraries of Barbaro and others in the city with a similar commission to search out Greek manuscripts for the Medici collection in Florence. Lascaris was to set up a Greek press in Florence which issued its first product,

the Hellenistic poems of the Planudean Anthology, in August 1494. This book and its immediate successors, printed on the presses of Lorenzo Alopa, made a striking attempt to avoid the intricacies of Greek cursive type by printing the entire text in inscriptional capitals. Lascaris's pupil and protégé Marcus Musurus was to become the chief editor of Aldine Greek texts. Aldus would hardly have failed to make contact with this commanding figure of Byzantine scholarship with whom he had so much in common, though no direct evidence of acquaintance survives before the turn of the century.

We are on scarcely more secure ground with Ermolao Barbaro. The eulogy of him as one of the leading lights of Venetian humanism in Aldus's first published work, the *Musarum Panagyris*, is a slender basis for estimating their relationship. This work ('the Assembly of the Muses') is a set of improving verses addressed to Alberto Pio. The chief point of it, however, seems to be the lengthy letter appended to it, addressed to Alberto's mother, and Pico's sister, Caterina Pio. Here, through the veil of flattery and flummery with which Renaissance aristocrats expected to be approached, he set out a programme which returns again and again to promotion of the study of Greek, as preparation for life, as the core of a rounded education. The occasion of this disquisition is said to be the presentation of a recently composed work on Greek accentuation.

The work was evidently printed several years after its composition, by the classical specialist de Tortis, perhaps about 1490. As a programme for the Pio boys it had already expired. The *Panagyris* and a similar brochure directed to Leonello Pio seem rather to have served as advertisements of Aldus's powers of composition and as specimens of his teaching methods. It is notable also for an extended passage holding up examples of cultured nobles for imitation: Federigo da Montefeltro (the famous book-loving condottiere), Pietro Barozzi (the Venetian humanist and bishop), and, most elaborately, Ermolao Barbaro, 'the glory of the Venetian senate'. Further evidence of the strong didactic turn of Aldus's mind lies in his *Latin Grammar*. This was likewise dedicated to Alberto Pio, and printed for Aldus in March 1493 on the presses of Andrea Torresani – a figure of great importance for the future. The epilogue expresses dissatisfaction with the elementary works currently available, and with the small rewards that grammar teachers could expect. There is a clear, but not precisely spelled out, desire to be of service to humanity in some greater cause, if only men of means could be persuaded to fund it.

What this greater cause was is no mystery. Throughout the early 1490s fairly regular mentions of Aldus crop up in connexion with the procuring and copying of texts. In 1491 Pico sent him, at his request, a Homer, though Pico's letter does not tell whether the 1488 edition or a manuscript is meant. He is mentioned in correspondence of the Hellenists Niccolò Leoniceno, Giorgio Valla

1
Detail of the Barbari map of Venice, a large aerial view of the city printed from six woodblocks in 1500. At the centre of the detail is the church and square of Sant'Agostino where Aldus had his printing house till 1506. The house itself, which Aldus called his *Thermae*, or baths, still stands in the Campo Sant'Agostino. *Reproduced by courtesy of the Trustees of the British Museum, Department of Prints and Drawings.*

and (at Bologna) Antonio Urceo as someone who could find Greek texts and have them transcribed. Aldus was now firmly inscribed in the circle of Venetian erudition which drew inspiration from the scientific, philosophical and philological studies of Ermolao Barbaro, since 1491 an exile at Rome (where he died in 1493). The act of imagination which is Aldus's first claim to fame lay in connecting the intense, encyclopaedic interests of these scholars with the great engines of the Venetian printing presses, the one to serve as the vehicle of the other. The unhindered view of antiquity implicit in Barbaro's acts of recuperation was to be realized in plain texts – texts which spoke for themselves, accurately printed, widely accessible, uncluttered by medieval commentary, the very symbol of that convergence of Greek and Latin culture through which understanding of the ancient world could be reached.

PREPARING TO PRINT

Doubtless Aldus continued to act as a teacher in this period, but to judge from the event, and from the six years' work that in 1497 he claimed to have spent preparing to print, he was at the same time laying the foundations of his venture by gathering manuscripts and editors and money. The first requirement was capital. The practical experience of having his own Latin grammar printed by Andrea Torresani had put him in touch with one of the leading printers of the city. Torresani was a man of much his own age, with a robust business sense formed as an employee of Nicholas Jenson in the 1470s. He played very safe in the texts he chose to print, earning a contemporary reputation for extreme personal meanness. But he could perhaps see in Aldus's proposal the possibility of long-term profit, if the goods were priced right, as indeed proved to be the case over the two decades of their partnership.

We know of the other underwriter of the venture only through the eventual winding up of the company in 1542. This person, though never named in any Aldine publication, was a backer as influential as any that Aldus could have found. From later, different testimony, we learn that Pierfrancesco Barbarigo, son and nephew of successive doges of Venice – his uncle Agostino was all-powerful till 1501 – put 'several thousand ducats' into the firm, sharing in due course perhaps half the profits, with Torresani and his junior partner Aldus taking the other half. Whether Alberto Pio, by now prince of Carpi in his own right, also contributed capital we do not know for certain: in the many fulsome prefaces addressed to him, it is difficult to disentangle the practical from the moral backing. But it seems beyond doubt from the dedication to Pio of all five parts of the Greek edition of Aristotle that the long years of preparation had some substantial support from him. At any rate, the arrangement with both

2
Constantinus Lascaris, *Erotemata*, an introduction to Greek grammar with a facing Latin translation The first publication of the Aldine press, finished on 8 March 1495
Original page-size 208×148 mm
G 7586, sig $a2^{v}$-a3

Barbarigo and Torresani can be shown to date back at least to 1495 Before then Aldus may have been dependent on Pio and on such goodwill as he could find from the class of persons complained of in the epilogue to the grammar of 1493 The most laborious of the preparations involved the engraving of punches and impression of matrices from them to make Greek type

An early sixteenth-century printer announced that he had secured the services of the craftsman who had cut all of Aldus's types, one Francesco da Bologna He is now satisfactorily identified as Francesco Griffo of Bologna, a goldsmith known as an engraver of letters from 1475 onwards The first decision to be made by Aldus, Francesco and the other advisers of the press (presumably including some of the Greek scribes and scholars whom Aldus had made it his business to cultivate) was the form and set of the letters. The earlier Venetian model of the press of Laonicus and Alexander, with its staggeringly redundant typecase based on old liturgical hands, or the Florentine model of Lascaris's inscriptional capitals, beautiful and clear but not easy to read over the long stretch, were not encouraging

Effective choice lay between the formalized script, stripped of the elaborations of handwriting, used in earlier Venetian Latin books for short passages of Greek, and current calligraphic hands It has generally been taken as a matter of regret that Aldus (or Griffo) settled on a specimen of the latter, specifically on a faithful reproduction of the cursive hand of the scribe Immanuel Rhusotas, as the researches of Nicolas Barker have made clear So influential were the Aldine books to become that this fount, and its increasingly smaller successors in the same style, imposed themselves on the European printing of Greek for hundreds of years. The attempt to capture the freedom and flow of contemporary handwriting in the rigidities of type was, in Victor Scholderer's words, 'directly counter to the very nature and genius of the printed page'. The real charge against the Aldine Greek founts is not ugliness (though to Proctor they were ugly), but want of legibility The fact that Aldus had the more difficult ligatures, contractions and combinations set out and explained on two pages of his first book – and this was no more than a selection from the 330 or so separate sorts of the first fount – is indicative in itself of the difficulties that readers must have felt at the time, and have ever since The wearisome overall effect may be compared to the misguided 'script' founts of computer typefaces nowadays, suitable for no more than a visiting card or invitation

With patrons and backers assembled, a supply of type and stocks of expensive paper laid in at his workshop in Campo Sant'Agostino (Fig.1), the technical expertise and possibly the actual presses of his partner Torresani at his service, the stage was at last set for Aldus to put his name to the books themselves Gutenberg in Germany and Sweynheym and Pannartz in Italy had made their

ἘΠΙΤΟΜΗ ΤΩΝ ὈΚΤΩ ΤΟΥ ΛΟΓΟΥ ΜΕΡΩΝ ΚΑΙ ἈΛΛΩΝ ΤΙΝΩΝ ἈΝΑΓΚΑΙΩΝ ΣΥΝΤΕΘΕΙΣΑ ΠΑΡΑ ΚΩΝΣΤΑΝΤΙΝΟΥ ΛΑΣΚΑΡΕΩΣ ΤΟΥ ΒΥΖΑΝΤΙΟΥ.

COMPENDIVM OCTO ORATIONIS PARTIVM ET ALIORVM QVORVNDAM NEcessariorum EDITVM A CONSTANTINO LASCARI BYZANTIO.

De diuisione literarum.

Liber primus.

Littera est pars minima uocis indiuidua. Sunt autem litterae uigintiquatuor. alpha. uita. gamma. delta. epsilo. zita. ita. thita. iota. cappa. labda. mi. gni. xi. omicron. pi. ro. sigma. taf. ypsilon. phi. chi. psi. omega. Harum uocales quidem septem. alpha. e psilon. ita. iota. omicron. ypsilon et omega. Consonantes autem decemseptem uita. gamma. delta. zita. thita. cappa. labda. mi. gni. xi. pi. ro. sigma. taf. phi. chi. psi. Sed uocalium longae quidem duae. ita et omega. Breues autem duae epsilon et omicron. Ancipites uero tres. alpha. iota. ypsilo.

beginnings with easily sold schoolbooks, in both cases the Donatus which formed the staple of late medieval grammar education. These served at the same time to advertise their craft and to support their larger enterprises. So too Aldus began with a grammar, programmatically a Greek accidence. Unlike nearly everything else he was to print in Greek, Constantine Lascaris's *Erotemata* was not an *editio princeps* with Aldus, having had the honour of being the first wholly Greek book ever printed (Milan, 1476, with several later editions). But Aldus had the wit to improve on earlier versions by supplying supplementary material in the form of a structured introduction to the Greek alphabet and some simple and familiar reading matter – the Lord's prayer, the opening of John's gospel, as well as a facing translation of the main text, 'useful, we believe, for those setting out on Greek' (Fig.2).

This first edition is dated in the Venetian style 28 February 1494, that is 1495

3
Musaeus, *Hero and Leander*, 1495–98. The preface refers to this as a precursor to the 1495 Aristotle, but the facing Latin version is printed in types not used before 1497: Aldus simply printed up a translation about 1498 and interleaved it with unsold copies of the Greek text. The woodcuts show two stages of Leander's tragic swim across the Hellespont. Original page-size 190×134 mm.
IA.24385, sig. b6v–b7.

Ἀντιπάτρου.
Οὗτος ὁ Λειάνδροιο διάπλοος· οὗτος ὁ πόντου
Πορθμὸς, ὁ μὴ μούνῳ τῷ φιλέοντι βαρύς.
Ταῦθ' Ἡροῦς τὰ πάροιθεν ἐπαύλια· τοῦτο τὸ πύργου
Λείψανον· ὧδ' ὁ προδότης τῷδ' ἐπέκειτο λύχνος.
Κοινὸς δ' ἀμφοτέρους ὅδ' ἔχει τάφος, εἰσέτι καὶ νῦν
Κείνῳ τῷ φθονερῷ μεμφομένους ἀνέμῳ.

Antipatri·

Hic eſt Leandri tranatus· hoc eſt ponti
Fretum non ſoli amanti graue.
Hæc Herûs antiquæ domicilia· hæ turris
Reliquiæ. proditrix hic pendebat lucerna.
Cómuneq; ambos hoc habet ſepulchrum, núc quoq;
De illo inuido conquerentes uento.

Clamabat tumidis audax Leander, í undis,
Parcite dú propo. mergite dú redeo.

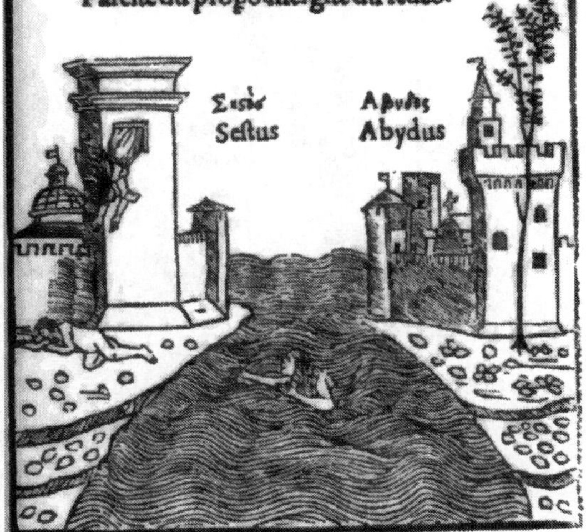

4
Aristotle, *Organon*, 1495
The first volume of the collected works of Aristotle, containing the treatises on logic, here annotated in the *Prior Analytics* by the sixteenth-century scholar Petrus Victorius (Pier Vettori)
Original page-size 311×210 mm
IB 24393, sig K4

in the common year, and the supplementary material 8 March 1495. It comes with two Latin prefaces and an epilogue which constitute the first statement we have of Aldus's aims. Several interesting points arise. The grammar is held out as a sample of greater things in store, a first, necessary step when there is such demand on all sides to learn Greek, and no books are now for sale that could meet the need. Aldus claims that the text is more correct than earlier editions, being based on a manuscript revised by the author himself and recently brought back from Messina in Sicily by the youthful Venetian nobles Pietro Bembo and Angelo Gabriele. As it happens the manuscript survives in the Vatican Library, and the claim can be shown to be false. Aldus in effect reprinted the edition (implicitly criticized) of Bonus Accursius (Milan, 1480), with sporadic interjection of glosses taken from Lascaris's revision, and the translation he said he supplied himself was no more than a lightly retouched version of that made and printed long before by Giovanni Crastoni. For all his many merits, Aldus was not above cutting corners and obscuring intellectual debts, particularly in his slighter pieces of printing. But he was by no means the inventor of the inexact publisher's blurb. The work ends with the promise that if studious youth would buy his work without delay, 'much more and much better' would be forthcoming.

Things had now reached a critical stage in the risky adventure on which Aldus and his partners were embarked. His next book, a Greek edition of the ancient (but not so ancient as was then believed) poem on Hero and Leander, attributed to the mythical poet Musaeus, repeats the brazen appeal for students to part with their money, in return – and here the programme becomes specific – he would be able to reward them with Aristotle and the other works of Greek wisdom (Fig 3). The Greek preface makes the ingenuous admission 'Without a great deal of money I cannot print.'

A sign of the financial strain involved in the undertaking lies in a document submitted to the Venetian senate three days before the first part of the Lascaris was printed, and evidently in urgent anticipation of that first publication. On 25 February 1495 Aldus applied for a privilege which would prevent anyone else reprinting or importing into Venetian territory any of the books, Greek or translations from Greek, which Aldus himself was designing to publish. And all this for a term of twenty years, in virtue of a new Greek type 'of the utmost beauty' and 'two new methods' of putting them to paper, in devising which he had used up 'a great part of his wealth'. It is not at all clear what these undefined 'secrets' were – probably the vertical kerning between lines and the method of printing the accents separately above the vowels to which they apply, so as to limit the number of sorts required to make up the fount. Nor is it clear whether Aldus was meaning to patent, as it were, the *design* of the typeface. But the

τι ἀληθὲς, οὔτε οὐκ ἀληθές. ὁμοίως δὲ καὶ ἐπὶ τῶν γ' δι· αἱ γὰρ ἀποφάσεις αἱ εἰρημέναι, δύο εἰσίν.

ΑΡΙΣΤΟΤΕΛΟΥΣ ΑΝΑΛΥΤΙΚΩΝ ΠΡΟΤΕΡΩΝ, ΔΕΥΤΕΡΟΝ.

Ἐν πόσοις μὲν οὖν σχήμασι καὶ διὰ ποίων καὶ πόσων προτάσεων, καὶ πότε, καὶ πῶς γίνεται συλλογισμὸς, ἔτι δὲ εἰς ποῖα βλεπτέον ἀνασκευάζοντι καὶ κατασκευάζοντι, καὶ πῶς δεῖ ζητεῖν περὶ τοῦ προκειμένου καθ' ὁποιανοῦν μέθοδον, ἔτι δὲ διὰ ποίας ὁδοῦ ληψόμεθα τὰς περὶ ἕκαστον ἀρχὰς, ἤδη διεληλύθαμεν. ἐπεὶ δ' οἱ μὲν καθόλου τῶν συλλογισμῶν εἰσὶν οἱ δὲ κατὰ μέρος, οἱ μὲν καθόλου πάντες ἀεὶ πλείω συλλογίζονται, τῶν δ' ἐν μέρει, οἱ μὲν κατηγορικοὶ, πλείω, οἱ δ' ἀποφατικοὶ τὸ συμπέρασμα μόνον. αἱ μὲν γὰρ ἄλλαι προτάσεις ἀντιστρέφουσιν, ἡ δὲ στερητικὴ οὐκ ἀντιστρέφει· τὸ δὲ συμπέρασμα, τὶ κατά τινός ἐστιν. ὥσθ' οἱ μὲν ἄλλοι συλλογισμοὶ πλείω συλλογίζονται. οἷον εἰ τὸ α δέδεικται παντὶ τῷ β, ἢ τινί, καὶ τὸ β τινὶ τῷ α ἀναγκαῖον ὑπάρχειν· καὶ εἰ μηδενὶ τῷ β τὸ α, οὐδὲ τὸ β οὐδενὶ τῷ α· τοῦτο δ' ἕτερον τοῦ ἔμπροσθεν. εἰ δὲ τὸ α τινὶ μὴ ὑπάρχει τῷ β, οὐκ ἀνάγκη καὶ τὸ β τινὶ τῷ α μὴ ὑπάρχειν· ἐνδέχεται γὰρ καὶ παντὶ ὑπάρχειν. αὕτη μὲν οὖν κοινὴ πάντων αἰτία, τῶν τε καθόλου καὶ τῶν κατὰ μέρος. ἔστι δὲ περὶ τῶν καθόλου καὶ ἄλλως εἰπεῖν. ὅσα γὰρ ἢ ὑπὸ τὸ μέσον ἢ ὑπὸ τὸ συμπέρασμά ἐστιν, ἁπάντων ἔσται ὁ αὐτὸς συλλογισμὸς, ἐὰν τὰ μὲν ἐν τῷ μέσῳ, τὰ δ' ἐν τῷ συμπεράσματι τεθῇ. οἷον εἰ τὸ α β συμπέρασμα,

5
Books for sale The first Aldine advertisement, giving minimum prices of everything printed in Greek up to 1 October 1498
Original page-size 357×245 mm
BN Paris, MS Grec 3064, fol 84
Reproduced by courtesy of the Bibliothèque Nationale de France

privilege granted him then was sufficient to see off rival printers of Greek books in 1498 when they attempted to issue books in a close copy of his fount, even if he could no longer at that stage rely on a monopoly of all Greek printing within the Venetian dominions The fragile undertaking of 1495 was by 1498 a sturdy business which no longer needed or justified this restraint of trade, thanks largely to Aldus's own success

PRINTING THE PHILOSOPHER

That success was founded on the Greek Aristotle (Fig 4) The separate editions issued over the four years 1495-98, each volume bearing an allusion to the privilege granted by the senate, were undoubtedly conceived as a series, though each was available by itself Aldus himself distinguished between the volume of logical works (the *Organon*, or 'instrument', so called from a poem prefixed to this edition) which was published in November 1495 and the later volumes of 'philosophy'. This was the real work which the partnership was set up to create The other Latin and Greek works of the earliest years were for the most part either quickly produced, easily sold educational texts, or in the nature of private press work for members of Aldus's intellectual and academic circle The five stout parts – often bound in six volumes owing to the great bulk of part IV – contain neither all of Aristotle nor only Aristotle. But 'the Aldine Aristotle' remains, in terms of the labour involved and the magnificence of the result, the greatest publishing venture of the fifteenth century The centrality of Aristotle in intellectual life of the time can hardly be overstressed In Latin dress he lay at the heart of any university course in philosophy, as dominant at the end of the Quattrocento as in the preceding three hundred years. The humanist return *ad fontes*, to the originals unobscured by imprecise translation and the encrustations of scholastic commentary, was the indispensable background to the edition. The call had been voiced for Aristotle in particular by Ermolao Barbaro; the climate he helped to create finds further reflection in the creation of a lectureship in Greek philosophy in the Venetian university at Padua in 1497 The new availability of the original text must also have played a part

Certain important Aristotelian works were as yet unfindable, notably the *Rhetoric* and the *Poetics* – Aldus was later to print the first Greek editions of both The second volume is largely taken up with the works of Theophrastus, the successor of Aristotle in the Athenian Lyceum This seems to have been on the advice of a scholastic philosopher at Padua named Francesco Cavalli, who wrote a treatise on the order in which Aristotle's works on natural philosophy were to be disposed, a treatise which Aldus was intending to print When we find the contents of the Aristotle specified in four volumes in an advertisement of 1498

¶LIBRI GRAECI IMPRESSI.

Haec sunt graecorum voluminum nomina, quae in Thermis Aldi Romani Venetiis impressa sunt ad hunc usq; diem .i. primum octobris M.IID. Nam cũ quotidie aliquis peteret, qui nam graeci libri formis excusi sint, ac quanti ueneant ad minimũ, quod uel ipse scire cuperet, uel ad amicos id cupide efflagitiis mitteret, pertaedebat toties idem scribere occupatissimum hominem.

¶In grammatica.

Erotemata Cõstantini Lascaris ex regione cũ interpretatione latina. ¶Item de literis, ac diphthõgis graecis. ¶Itẽ introductio quaedam docens etiã sine magistro syllabas & dictiões graecas posse legere, tã paruis q̃ maiusculis scriptas characteribus. ¶Item quo nam modo literae & diphthõgi graecae ad nos ueniant. ¶Item abbreuiationes q̃ plurimae, quibus frequentissime graeci utũtur. ¶Item Pater noster. ¶Aue Maria. ¶Salue Regina. ¶Credo in unum deũ patrem omnipotẽtem. ¶In pricipio erat uerbum. ¶Itẽ aurea carmina Pythagorae. ¶Itẽ Poema Phocylidae utilissima. omnia cũ expositione latina e regiõe i uno uolumine uẽdunt marcellis quatuor.

Grammatica Urbani utilissima ad declinãda nomina, pronomina, & uerba omnia tã linguae cõis, q̃ aliarũ quatuor. Attica. Ionica. Dorica. Aeolica. cũ regulis optimis & necessariis ita, ut nihil ferẽ sit praetermissum, quod introducere posse i graecam linguã uisum fuerit. Ubi etiam copiose tractatur de caeteris orationis partibus. Venditur nõ minoris marcellis quatuor.

Canonismata quae thesaurus & cornucopiae appellãtur dictionum difficilium, & maxime uerborum, quae apud Homerum ex commentariis Eustathii, & aliorum grammaticorum per ordinem literarũ. ¶Aelii Dionysii de indeclinabilibus uerbis. ¶Declinationes uerborũ sum & eo, utilissimae. ¶De iis quae sedere significant. ¶Quot sint quae ire significant. ¶Ex scriptis Herodiani excerpta de magno uerbo scitu dignissima, & rara inuentu. ¶Ex scriptis eiusdẽ deductiones uerborum difficulter declinatorum. ¶Choerobosci ad eos qui in omnibus uerbis regulas quaerunt & similitudines. ¶Eiusdem in quibus ob malesonantiam attrahatur n litera. ¶De anomalis & inaequalibus uerbis secũdum ordinem alphabeti. ¶Herodiani de inclinatis, & encliticis & coencliticis dictiunculis. ¶Ex scriptis Choerobosci de iis quae iclinantur, encliticisq;. ¶Sine auctore de iis quae inclinãtur. ¶Ex scriptis Ioannis grammatici de idiomatis. ¶Eustathii de idiomatis quae apud Homerũ. ¶Itẽ de idiomatis, ex iis quae a Corintho decerpta. ¶De foemininis noibus, quae desinunt in o magnum. oĩa in uno uolumine. Vendũtur minimo, nummo aureo & semis.

Grammatica doctissima & (pace aliorum dixerim) omnium utilissima Theodori Gazae uiri ingenio & doctrina uel cum antiquissimis conferendi. ¶Eiusdem de mẽsibus pulcherrimum opus. ¶Item quatuor libri Appollonii de cõstructiõe. Omnia i uno uolumine. Veneunt aureo nummo, nec minoris.

Dictionarium graecum copiosissimum secundum ordinem alphabeti cum interpretatione latina. ¶Cyrilli opusculum de dictionibus, quae uariato accentu mutant significatum secundum ordinem alphabeti cum interpretatione latina. ¶Ammonius de differentia dictionum per literarum ordinem. ¶Vetus istructio & denominatiões perfectorum militũ. ¶Significata τοῦ ἤ. ¶Significata τοῦ ὡς. ¶Index oppido q̃ copiosus per literarũ latinarũ ordinẽ, quod est loco dictionarii latini copiosissimi cum interpretatione graeca. Docet n. latinas dictiões ferẽ omneis graece dicere, & multas et multis modis. Omnes in uno uolumine minimum pretiũ est aureus nummus.

¶In Poetica.

Theocriti ecloge triginta. ¶Hesiodi theogonia. ¶Eiusdẽ scutum herculis. ¶Eiusdẽ georgicorum libri duo. ¶Maximi Planudae ex latino libro qui Cato dicitur Sniae paraeneticae distichi. ¶Caput De inuidia. Theognidis Megarẽsis siculi sniae elegiacae. ¶Sniae per capita monostichi per capita ex uariis poetis. Aurea Carmina Pythagorae. ¶Phocylidae poema admonitoriũ utilissimũ. ¶Carmina Sibyllae erythreae de christo IESV. ¶Differẽtia uocũ. Omnia in uno uolumine. Venduntur non minoris marcellis octo.

Aristophanis cum antiquis commentariis Comoediae nouem. Plutus. Nebulae. Ranae. Equites. Acharnes. Vespae. Aues. Pax. Cõtionatrices foeminae. Minimum pretiũ ueneũt, aurei nũmi duo & semis.

Musaei poetae antiquissimi De Herone & Leandro amantibus cum interpretatione latina. uenditur, marcello.

¶In logica.

Logica Aristotelis i. organũ. hoc est Porphyrii introductio siue uniuersalia liber unus. ¶Praedicamẽta Aristotelis liber unus. ¶Periermenias liber unus, siue sectiones sex. ¶Priora resolutoria libri duo. ¶Posteriora resolutoria libri duo. ¶Topica libri octo. ¶Elenchi libri duo. Oẽs i uno uolumine uẽdũtur aureo & semis.

In philosophia. Primum uolumen.

Vita Aristotelis p Laertiũ & philoponũ & uita Theophrasti. ¶Aristotelis physicorũ libri octo. ¶De coelo libri quatuor. ¶De gñatiõe & corruptiõe libri duo. ¶Meteorologicorũ libri quatuor. ¶De mũdo ad Alexãdrũ liber unus & Philõis iudaei de mũdo liber un⁹. ¶Theophrasti de igne liber unus. ¶De uẽtis liber unus. ¶De lapidibus liber unus. ¶De signis aquarũ & uẽtorũ icerti auctoris. Oẽs i uno uolumine uẽdũtur ad minimũ nũmis aureis duobus.

¶Secundum uolumen.

De historia aĩalium libri octo. ¶De ptibus animaliũ libri quatuor. ¶De gressu aĩalium liber unus. ¶De aĩa libri tres. ¶De sensu liber unus. ¶De memoria liber unus. ¶De somno & uigilia liber unus. ¶De somniis liber unus. ¶De diuinatione per somnium liber unus. ¶De motu aĩalium liber unus. ¶De gñatione aĩalium, libri qnq;. ¶De longitudine & breuitate uitae liber unus. ¶De iuuẽtute & senectute, & respiratiõe, & uita & morte libri tres. ¶De spiritu liber unus. ¶De coloribus liber unus. ¶Physiognomicorum liber unus. ¶De mirabilibus auditiõibus liber unus. ¶De Xenophanis Zenonis & Gorgiae opiõibus, liber unus. ¶De idiuisibilibus lineis, liber unus. ¶Theophrasti de piscibus liber unus. ¶De uertigine oculorũ liber unus. ¶De laboribus, liber unus. ¶De odoribus, liber unus. ¶De sudoribus, liber unus. oẽs in uno uolumine minimum pretium Venetiis nummi aurei duo & semis.

¶Tertium Volumen.

Theophrasti de historia plãtarũ, libri decẽ. ¶Eiusdẽ de causis plantarũ libri sex. ¶Aristotelis problematum sectiões duodequadraginta. ¶Alexandri aphrodisiẽsis problematũ libri duo. ¶Aristotelis mechanicorũ liber unus. ¶Eiusdẽ metaphysicorũ libri quatuordecim. ¶Theophrasti metaphysicorũ liber unus. Oẽs in uno uolumine minimũ pretium nummi aurei, tres.

¶Quartum Volumen.

Aristotelis magnorũ moraliũ ad Nicomachũ patrẽ libri duo. ¶Ethicorũ ad Eudemum discipulum libri octo. ¶Ethicorũ ad Nicomachum filium libri decẽ. ¶Oeconomicorũ libri duo. ¶Politicorũ libri octo. oẽs i eodẽ uolumie minimum pctiũ nũmi aurei duo.

Psalterium graecum. uendĩ marcellis quatuor.

In sacra scriptura.

Officium in honorẽ Beatissimae uirginis cum psalmis penitentialibus e latino in graecum. uenditur Marcellis duobus.

6
Comoediae of Aristophanes, 1498. The first publication of the masterpieces of Athenian comedy, edited by the Cretan scholar Marcus Musurus. This page shows the opening of *The Frogs*. The text is set in the first Aldine greek type, fringed by the collection of ancient explanations known as *Scholia* in the second Aldine greek. Original page-size 316×210 mm
c 8674, sig λ3

(with the logical works classed separately), that probably reflects the intellectual structure rather than the chronological appearance of the set (Fig 5).

Aldus had many other helpers beside Cavalli. Griffo may have been called upon to supply new sorts when the Lascaris type was recast on a larger body, with an increase in contractions and abbreviations. Scholars came from the university milieu. Thomas Linacre, 'an Englishman most learned in Latin and Greek', is thanked among others in the preface to the second volume of Aristotle (Linacre owned, no doubt thanks to this editorial work, the only known complete set of the Aristotle printed on vellum, an extraordinary treasure now in New College, Oxford). Two learned Greeks displaced by political turmoil in Florence, Marcus Musurus and Aristobulus Apostolis, were editors and contributors to the press from 1495. We have from 1498 an interesting picture, drawn by Musurus in a Greek letter, of the exacting labour of correcting proof in the Aldine office: mistakes of the compositors swarmed before the eyes like heads of the Hydra – as soon as one was cut off more appeared.

These and other Greek scholars were employed on more than correcting proof. They helped in the first place to gather and compare the manuscripts needed for the editions; they wrote out fair copies to spare the precious manuscripts from the markings of the compositors – not often enough, it must be said, they corrected the text of an author before and through the press. The search for copy took Aldus's letters all over Europe, as far, he said, as distant Britain. Even the Aristotle was held up in its last volume as he tried to obtain Greek manuscripts of works known only in Latin translation. Of some texts it was a triumph to secure even one copy. We must not ask of Aldine editions what they cannot give, a balanced critical recension which even in our own day has hardly been achieved for many Greek authors. The aims of textual purity and correctness were often trumpeted in early editions, long before Aldus, indeed, but with special emphasis in his prefaces. But these aims, no doubt genuinely held, all too frequently succumbed to the messy pressures of the printing house, as the number of *errata* pages attached to his editions attest. Something is better than nothing, Aldus says in the preface to Theocritus in 1496, and a text once printed can at least find many correctors where a manuscript can only receive occasional emendation. This of course is true in the long run, but sidesteps the whole problem of corrupt texts being fixed in hundreds of copies by the printing press. We can turn to a candid critic of Aldus, his close friend Antonio Urceo, to examine contemporary reaction.

Urceo, professor of Latin and Greek at Bologna, had already helped Aldus with the preparations for the Theocritus, by seeking out codices and offering explanations of a textual crux. When the third part of the Aristotle appeared early in 1498, Urceo wrote to another friend that he was overjoyed to have it,

ἈΡΙΣΤΟΦΆΝΟΥΣ ΒΆΤΡΑΧΟΙ

ΞΑΝΘΊΑΣ ὈΡΡΟΛΟΓΊΖΩΝ.

ΔΙ.

Εἴπω τι τῶν εἰωθότων ὦ δέσποτα,
Ἐφ' οἷς ἀεὶ γελῶσιν οἱ θεώμενοι;
Δι. Νὴ τὸν Δί' ὅτι βούλει γε, πλὴν πιέζομαι.
Τοῦτο δὲ φύλαξαι· πάνυ γάρ ἐστ' ἤδη χολή.
Ξα. Μηδ' ἕτερον ἀστεῖόν τι; Δι. πλήν γ' ὡς θλίβομαι.
Ξα. Τί δαί; τὸ πάνυ γέλοιον εἴπω; Δι. νὴ Δία.
Θαρρῶν γ'· ἐκεῖνο μόνον ὅπως μὴ 'ρεῖς. Ξα. τὸ τί;
Δι. Μεταβαλλόμενος τἀνάφορον, ὅτι χεζητιᾷς.
Ξα. Μηδ' ὅτι τοσοῦτον ἄχθος ἐπ' ἐμαυτῷ φέρων,
Εἰ μὴ καθαιρήσει τις, ἀποπαρδήσομαι;
Δι. Μὴ δῆθ' ἱκετεύω, πλήν γ' ὅταν μέλλω 'ξεμεῖν.

Εἴπω τι τῶν εἰωθότων. [illegible] Ὅμηρος [illegible]
Νὴ Δί' ὅτι βούλει γε. [illegible]
Πάνυ γάρ ἐστ' ἤδη χολή. [illegible] Γέλοιον. [illegible]

[illegible] Μεταβαλλόμενος [illegible]
[illegible]
Μηδ' ὅτι τοσοῦτον. [illegible] Ἀποπαρδήσομαι. [illegible]
[illegible] Πλήν γ' ὅταν μέλλω 'ξεμεῖν. [illegible]
[illegible]

Nemesim. quæ & læda dr (ut refert Crates tragœdia pr scriptor) quæ enim é ouú uñ nata é Helena. sed quoniam Iupiter rursus i cœlũ i cygnũ tali figuratus se recepit, Vt fuit pẽnis tẽsus simulacrum eius syderibus reliq. Habet autem stellas in capite claram unam. in dextra ala quinq. unã claram quæ é erga collum. in sinistra ala quinq. in pectore unam. in cauda unam, quæ é amplissima. Sunt oés. xiii.

AQVARIVS

o Ceano mersus sopitas condere flammas.
Himbres occasus ortusq; intercepit ora.
Et cum terrores auget mox atra marinos,
Multum clamatos frustra spectaueritortus,
Tunc rigor, aut rapidus ponto tunc incubat auster.
Tarda ministeria & nautis tremor alligat artus
Et rationem animi temeraria pectora soluent.
Nulla dies oritur, quæ iam uacua æquora cernat.
Puppibus & semper tumidis ratis innatet undis,
Interea tentare undas iuuat, aspera sed cum
Assultat lateri deprensæ spuma carinæ,
Tunc alti curuos prospectant littore portus.
Inuentasq; alii terras pro munere narrant,
Interea exanimat pauidos instantis aquæ mons:
Ast alii procul e terra iactantur in altum.
Munit & hos breue lignum, & fata instantia pellit,
Et tantum a leto, quantum rate fluctibus absunt.

an invaluable aid to his teaching. But two aspects dismayed him, the very high cost of the volume, for which he could have got ten good Latin books, and the fact that the misprints were so frequent that he was often in a quandary as to whether they were actual errors or simply terms unknown to him. He expresses surprise that the Greeks in Aldus's employ could have let such damaging nonsense go by.

All this casts doubt on the general accuracy of Aldine texts, doubts which modern research has tended to back in detail. In the rare instances that we can examine the manuscripts collated for use at the press, or actually used as printer's copy, the process of correction seems bewilderingly haphazard. Emendation is casual and as often wrong as right, the results very often imperfectly communicated to the pressmen. It seems that commercial pressures, the need to get saleable products onto the bookstalls, overwhelmed the scholarly care we might have expected from the tone and statements of the prefaces. It is in any case true that Greek philology, even among Greeks as expert as Musurus, had not advanced far enough to deal with the large scale corruption carried by late Byzantine manuscripts.

Urceo also raises the question of the price of Aldus's products. Good fortune has preserved in a single copy in Paris an advertisement which Aldus had printed in the same year, 1498, that saw the completion of the Aristotle, and thus the initial programme of the partnership (Fig.5). By now there were many other Aldine editions on sale, and from account books of the Barbarigo family we can deduce a rough division into works produced for the partnership, works printed by Aldus on his own account (*i.e.*, at his own cost and risk), and those printed on commission for others. The advertisement dated 1 October 1498 sets out only those books printed in Greek which were available for sale at Venice. Though the list has uses for dating individual editions and instructive absences – works which we know to have been printed but which are not offered for sale – its main interest lies in the scale of minimum prices given for each book: minimum, because that was the price at source, in Aldus's shop and presumably also in Torresani's elsewhere in the city, without binding or illumination or whatever else buyers might want in order to individualize their copies.

The prices no doubt bore some relation to the labour involved, and Aldus constantly stresses the difficulties of getting hold of and setting up in type these Greek texts. But they were seen as expensive at the time, by others besides Urceo; and well into the sixteenth century, as late as 1547, apparently new sets of Aristotle were still available for sale. In 1525 Erasmus ordered a set from the heirs of Aldus. In his own edition of Aristotle of 1531 – the second printing in Greek, none having been called for in the interval – he remarked that the cost of the Aldine had always been a bar to poor students of philosophy. The five

7
Aquarius from the *Astronomici Veteres*, 1499. The woodcuts of the constellations were re-used blocks from Venetian astronomical editions of the 1480s. Original page-size 301×208 mm. IB.24484, sig. H7^v^.

8
A page of the *Miscellanea* of Angelo Poliziano, from the *Opera* of the Florentine humanist published in 1498. In his discussion of ancient worship, Poliziano includes a quotation from the Hebrew Psalms in order to correct an error in the Septuagint translation: the words represent Aldus's first attempt at Hebrew type. Original page-size 320×224 mm. IB 24473, sig. H8

volumes were offered in 1498 at a total of eleven ducats, the most substantial part (IV) alone costing three ducats. Comparisons in this area are notoriously difficult, but the monthly wage of a compositor in a printing house might be three or four ducats, the Vatican librarian earned ten ducats a month, a schoolmaster might make fifty ducats per year, a well-paid humanities professor as much as a hundred and fifty ducats. Where we can compare similar works on sale at Venetian booksellers of the time, usually in the lower range of grammars and dictionaries, Aldine prices are often twice as high. The books were available, but they were not cheap.

AFTER ARISTOTLE

Besides the Aristotle, which in itself outweighed in sheer number of pages all Greek ever printed before, by 1498 Aldus had put out a few works of a literary kind. But the intent was not so much literary as didactic and linguistic. Greek texts were presented as a means of opening up the stores of Greek learning, still in many areas valid guides to the sciences. The edition of Hesiod and Theocritus was printed in February 1496 at the request of his old teacher Battista Guarino, who wished to lecture on these texts at Ferrara. Aristophanes, edited by Marcus Musurus in 1498 (Fig. 6), was recommended by Aldus as a guide to pure spoken Attic Greek, not for any literary or even comic quality – though Musurus spoke of it as light relief from a diet of Aristotle. Aldus's preface to the edition insists, rather oddly in the context but in essence repeating the call first heard in the prefaces to Aristotle, on the absolute necessity of Greek for access to the disciplines of rhetoric and dialectic, mathematics and medicine, and all branches of philosophy.

In this regard Aldine production diverged sharply from the continuing series of literary texts issuing from Alopa's press in Florence – the Greek Anthology, Callimachus, Lucian, Apollonius Rhodius, as well as some texts of a more practical nature. The market Aldus had in view was resolutely academic, and this extended to a large sector of his Latin publications too. It might seem to us that the Neoplatonic commentaries translated into Latin by Marsilio Ficino (September 1497) would not have found a wide acceptance, but Aldus was told precisely the opposite in an encouraging letter sent him by the poet Ariosto soon after its appearance. The collection of Greek and Latin astronomical texts (not clearly distinguished from astrological works) which appeared in 1499 was also undoubtedly intended for university instruction. A set of rather crude woodcuts of the star figures adorns Aratus in this collection, one of the few occasions that Aldus deigned to publish an illustrated book (Fig. 7).

A special case was the *Opera omnia* of Politian (Fig. 8). Apart from the poet

potius ac moderatorem. Ex quo etiam digito labra comprimit, argumentum taciturnitatis & silentii. Quin mense eo, quem uocant Mesorem, primitias leguminum offerentes, ita dictitant, lingua, fortuna, lingua dæmon, déq; ægyptiacis arboribus, persicam in primis ei sacratam ferunt, Quod fructus cordi, frons linguæ, persimilis. Hactenus ex Plutarcho de Harpocrate, carptim, uellicatimq;, & per interualla. Meminit eiusdem Lucilius quoq; poeta græcus in epigrammate ad Dionysium, monens ut si quem habeat inimicum, nec Isin ei, nec Harpocratem, aut qui cæcos deus faciat iratos precetur, cogniturũ quid Deus, quid Simo ualeat. Sed & Tertullianus in Apologetico, sic ait. Serapidem & Isidem, & Harpocratem, cum suo cynocephalo, capitolio ꝓhibitos inferri, idest curia deorum pulsos, Piso & Gabinius cõsules, nõ utiq; Christiani, euersis etiam aris eorum abdicauerunt, turpiũ & ociosarum superstitionum uitia cohibentes, his uos restitutis summam maiestatem contulistis. M. autem Varro in libro de latina lingua ita scribit Cælum & terra, hi dei iidẽ qui ægypti Serapis, & Isis, & si Harpocrates digito significat, ut taceas. De hoc igitur intellexit Ouidius libro Metamorphoseon nono,

Sanctáq; Bubastis, uariísq; coloribus apis
Quíq; premit uocem, digitóq; silentia suadet.

Etiam Augustinus libro de ciuitate dei undeuigesimo, Et quoniam (inquiens) ferè in omnibus templis ubi colebantur Isis & Serapis, erat etiam simulachrũ, quod digito labiis impresso, admonere uideretur, ut silentium fieret, hoc significare idem Varro existimat, ut homines eos fuisse tacerent. Hactenus Augustinus. Sed in epistola Abammonis ægyptii ad Porphyrium, quam aut in græcam uertisse orationem, aut etiam composuisse Platõicus Iamblichus existimatur de deo quodam, ubi secundo fit mentio, cui nomen ægyptiaca lingua fecerit Icheõ, hunc ostendit silentio coli oportere. Quod idem etiam de summi dei cultu prolixe Porphyrius ἐν τῷ περὶ ζώων ἀποχῆς Quin Dauid item propheta psalmum ita quempiam inchoat.

לך דומיה תהלה אלהים בציו

lecha dumiã tehilã elohim bezion.

Id latine significat, Tibi silentium laus, deus in Sion. Quod aliter tamen interpretes septuaginta uerterunt, hoc est.

Te decet hymnus deus in Sion.

Quare Harpocratem puto ægyptii suis adhibebant sacris, qui silentio colendum ostenderet, summum deorum. Plinius quoq; de Harpo-

9
Psalter in Greek, about 1498
The title page with one of Aldus's rare woodcut borders, showing in the right margin King David with his harp. The text is printed with capital letters in red to give a traditional liturgical look.
Original page-size 213×153 mm
IA 24458, sig α3

Giannantonio Campano and his own friend Giovanni Pico, Politian was the first contemporary author to have his works gathered together in this way. For Aldus it was something of a departure: previous to this edition of 1498 he had printed in Latin only the Ficino edition and occasional pieces by friends (Bembo's dialogue *De Aetna* and Alessandro Benedetti's *Diaria de bello Carolino* in 1496, along with relatively short texts by his medical colleagues and helpers on the Aristotle, Lorenzo Maioli and Niccolò Leoniceno in 1497). The Politian was a much bigger job than any of these, 452 leaves, but fortunately the hard work of assembling the scattered philological papers of the great humanist had been done by his devoted coterie at Florence and Bologna. Indeed, the project was to have been printed by the Bolognese printer Platone Benedetti, who had been involved in the publication of Politian's separate works since the early 1490s. But at Benedetti's death in August 1496 the edition had probably not progressed much beyond the single sheet which has recently come to light. Here then was a ready-made prestige edition for a scholarly publisher such as Aldus had already proved himself to be, one that required a fair amount of Greek and a small quantity of Hebrew. For his part Aldus could add some material deriving from the papers of Ermolao Barbaro and the letters he had exchanged with Politian in 1484. Apparently with Aldus's acquiescence, the editor Alessandro Sarti retouched these letters with favourable mentions of himself.

Two other small works of this period stand outside the normal run of production. Without prefaces from Aldus himself, they are probably works commissioned by, or at least for the use of, the Uniate Greek community in Venice and the Venetian dominions. But the Greek Psalter (Figs 9 – 11) and miniature Greek Book of Hours (Fig. 12), both of 1497 – 98, may have had a pedagogic purpose too. Politian himself said he had learned Greek by studying a bilingual Bible, and the familiarity of the liturgical content to Latin speakers lent itself to use in these books as simple readers for beginners. A further clue is the very rare introduction to Greek *(Brevissima introductio ad litteras graecas)*, like the Hours in 16° format and bound with it in three copies now in Paris and New York. The two opuscula seem designed for one another's company, evidently for the use of Latin readers.

CHANGING DIRECTION: LATIN AND VERNACULAR

As we reach 1499, a change in the editorial direction of the Aldine press begins to be observed. Certainly Aldus could still produce in that year two wholly Greek texts very much in the erudite tradition of Barbaro and Venetian humanism: the medical works of Dioscorides and Nicander, and a collection of the Greek epistolographers dedicated to his friend Urceo. But he had promised

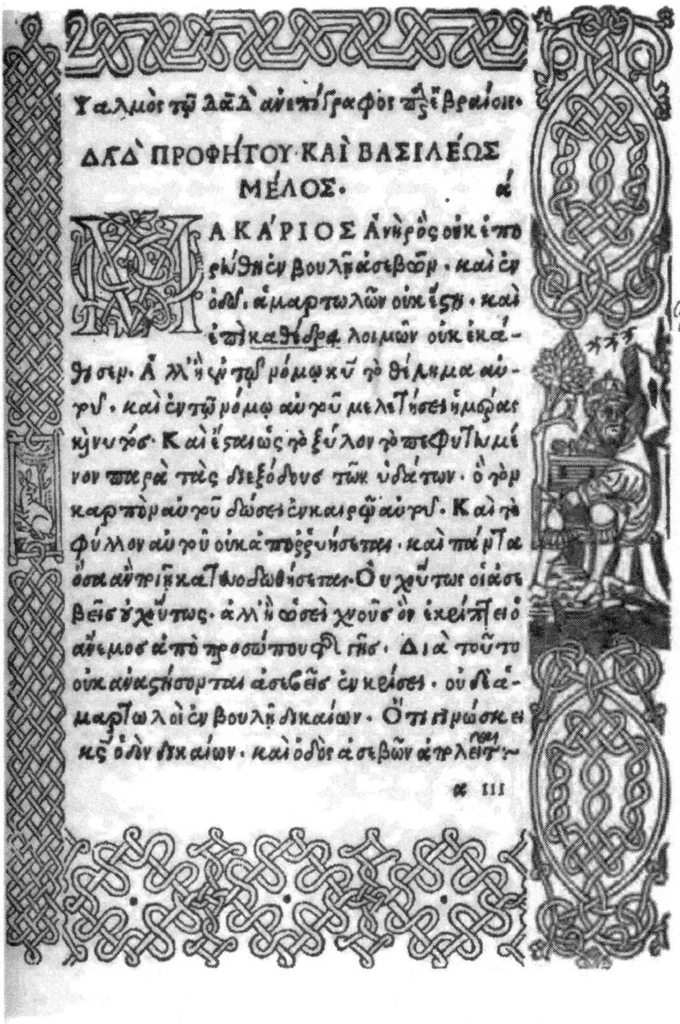
Ψαλμὸς τῷ Δαυὶδ ἀνεπίγραφος παρ' Ἑβραίοις.

ΔΑΥΙΔ ΠΡΟΦΗΤΟΥ ΚΑΙ ΒΑΣΙΛΕΩΣ
ΜΕΛΟΣ. α'

ΜΑΚΑΡΙΟΣ ἀνὴρ ὃς οὐκ ἐπο-
ρεύθη ἐν βουλῇ ἀσεβῶν· καὶ ἐν
ὁδῷ ἁμαρτωλῶν οὐκ ἔστη· καὶ
ἐπὶ καθέδρᾳ λοιμῶν οὐκ ἐκά-
θισεν. Ἀλλ' ἢ ἐν τῷ νόμῳ κυρίου τὸ θέλημα αὐ-
τοῦ· καὶ ἐν τῷ νόμῳ αὐτοῦ μελετήσει ἡμέρας
καὶ νυκτός. Καὶ ἔσται ὡς τὸ ξύλον τὸ πεφυτευμέ-
νον παρὰ τὰς διεξόδους τῶν ὑδάτων· ὃ τὸν
καρπὸν αὐτοῦ δώσει ἐν καιρῷ αὐτοῦ. Καὶ τὸ
φύλλον αὐτοῦ οὐκ ἀπορρυήσεται· καὶ πάντα
ὅσα ἂν ποιῇ κατευοδωθήσεται. Οὐχ οὕτως οἱ ἀσεβεῖς οὐχ οὕτως· ἀλλ' ἢ ὡσεὶ χνοῦς ὃν ἐκρίπτει ὁ
ἄνεμος ἀπὸ προσώπου τῆς γῆς. Διὰ τοῦτο
οὐκ ἀναστήσονται ἀσεβεῖς ἐν κρίσει· οὐδὲ ἁ-
μαρτωλοὶ ἐν βουλῇ δικαίων. Ὅτι γινώσκει
κύριος ὁδὸν δικαίων· καὶ ὁδὸς ἀσεβῶν ἀπολεῖται.

α iii

10–11
After the passage through the press of most of the sheets of the Greek *Psalter* it was noticed that a line of Psalm 72 ('He shall have dominion also from sea to sea') had been inadvertently omitted. In most copies the verse was written in by hand in the printing house. The remaining sheets of the run had the first few lines reset in a smaller type so as to squeeze in the omitted matter. The plates show sig. ι1 of C.9.a.2 with manuscript addition and G.12028 with reset type. Original page-size 200×131 mm (C.9.a.2) and 204×144 mm (G.12028).

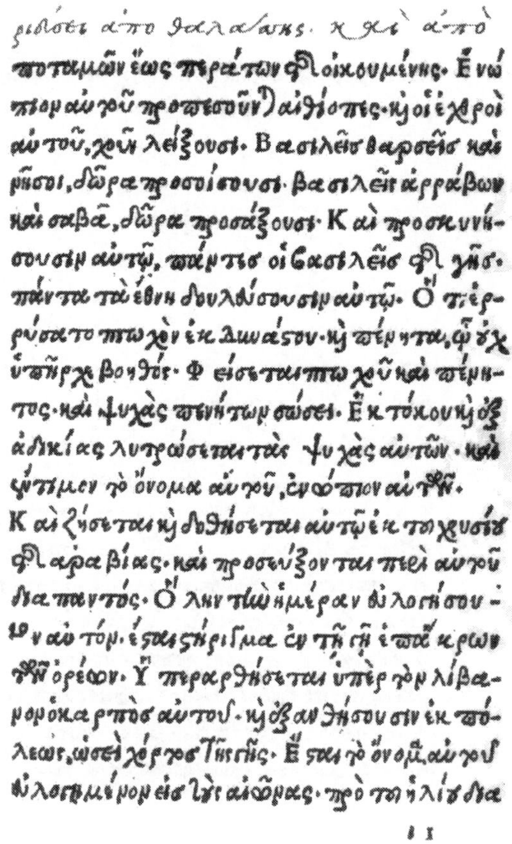
ριεύσει ἀπὸ θαλάσσης. καὶ ἀπὸ
ποταμῶν ἕως περάτων τῆς οἰκουμένης. Ἐνώπιον αὐτοῦ προπεσοῦνται αἰθίοπες. καὶ οἱ ἐχθροὶ
αὐτοῦ, χοῦν λείξουσι. Βασιλεῖς θαρσεῖς καὶ
νῆσοι, δῶρα προσοίσουσι. βασιλεῖς ἀράβων
καὶ σαβᾶ, δῶρα προσάξουσι. Καὶ προσκυνή-
σουσιν αὐτῷ, πάντες οἱ βασιλεῖς τῆς γῆς.
πάντα τὰ ἔθνη δουλεύσουσιν αὐτῷ. Ὅτι ἐρ-
ρύσατο πτωχὸν ἐκ δυνάστου. καὶ πένητα, ᾧ οὐχ
ὑπῆρχε βοηθός. Φείσεται πτωχοῦ καὶ πένη-
τος. καὶ ψυχὰς πενήτων σώσει. Ἐκ τόκου καὶ ἐξ
ἀδικίας λυτρώσεται τὰς ψυχὰς αὐτῶν. καὶ
ἔντιμον τὸ ὄνομα αὐτοῦ, ἐνώπιον αὐτῶν.
Καὶ ζήσεται καὶ δοθήσεται αὐτῷ ἐκ τοῦ χρυσίου
τῆς ἀραβίας. καὶ προσεύξονται περὶ αὐτοῦ
διαπαντός. Ὅλην τὴν ἡμέραν εὐλογήσου-
σιν αὐτόν. ἔσται στήριγμα ἐν τῇ γῇ ἐπ' ἄκρων
τῶν ὀρέων. Ὑπεραρθήσεται ὑπὲρ τὸν λίβα-
νον ὁ καρπὸς αὐτοῦ. καὶ ἐξανθήσουσιν ἐκ πό-
λεως, ὡσεὶ χόρτος τῆς γῆς. Ἔσται τὸ ὄνομα αὐτοῦ
εὐλογημένον εἰς τοὺς αἰῶνας. πρὸ τοῦ ἡλίου δια
ι ι

ριεύσει ἀπὸ θαλάσσης ἕως θαλάσσης καὶ ἀπὸ ποταμοῦ ἕως πε
ράτων τῆς οἰκουμένης. Ἐνώπιον αὐτοῦ προπεσοῦνται αἰθίοπες:
καὶ οἱ ἐχθροὶ αὐτοῦ λείξουσι. Βασιλεῖς θαρσεῖς καὶ
νῆσοι, δῶρα προσοίσουσι· βασιλεῖς ἀῤῥάβων
καὶ σαβᾶ, δῶρα προσάξουσι· Καὶ προσκυνή-
σουσιν αὐτῷ, πάντες οἱ βασιλεῖς τῆς γῆς·
πάντα τὰ ἔθνη δουλεύσουσιν αὐτῷ. Ὅτι ἐρ-
ρύσατο πτωχὸν ἐκ δυνάστου, καὶ πένητα, ᾧ οὐχ
ὑπῆρχε βοηθός· Φείσεται πτωχοῦ καὶ πένη-
τος, καὶ ψυχὰς πενήτων σώσει. Ἐκ τόκου καὶ ἐξ
ἀδικίας λυτρώσεται τὰς ψυχὰς αὐτῶν, καὶ
ἔντιμον τὸ ὄνομα αὐτοῦ, ἐνώπιον αὐτῶν.
Καὶ ζήσεται καὶ δοθήσεται αὐτῷ ἐκ τοῦ χρυσίου
τῆς ἀραβίας. καὶ προσεύξονται περὶ αὐτοῦ
διὰ παντός. Ὅλην τὴν ἡμέραν εὐλογήσου-
σιν αὐτόν. ἔσται στήριγμα ἐν τῇ γῇ ἐπ' ἄκρων
τῶν ὀρέων. Ὑπεραρθήσεται ὑπὲρ τὸν λίβα-
νον ὁ καρπὸς αὐτοῦ· καὶ ἐξανθήσουσιν ἐκ πό-
λεως, ὡσεὶ χόρτος τῆς γῆς. Ἔσται τὸ ὄνομα αὐτοῦ
εὐλογημένον εἰς τοὺς αἰῶνας. πρὸ τοῦ ἡλίου δια

ι ι

12
Greek *Hours of the Virgin Mary*, 1497 A little prayer-book for Greek exiles, printed in black and red The cut of the Annunciation was from a block used by another printer for a Latin Book of Hours in 1493
Original page-size 112×74 mm
G 12135, sig $\alpha 1^{v}$-$\alpha 2$

much more in this line, as early as 1497 the works of Plato in Greek, and even earlier a whole series of the ancient Aristotelian commentators. The problem seems to have been that the original Greek texts in their expensive folios were very welcome to very few Perhaps no more than five per cent of Italians with a humanist education (that is, in the classics) could really get to grips with unadorned – in places unintelligibly corrupt – Greek texts, when they could, as in the case of Antonio Urceo, the blemishes leaped to the eye The professional philosophers of the north Italian universities were in general not humanist by training and were not easy to wean from their medieval Latin Aristotle, with all its accumulated weight of still active Averroistic commentary. Torresani himself had taken part in the printing of a huge collected Latin Aristotle in the 1480s and was still publishing a great deal of scholastic Aristotelian commentary on his own account even while sharing in Aldus's enterprise He knew what would sell

A straw in the wind was the need to equip, probably around 1498, the early Musaeus with a facing Latin translation. Another may have been the abandonment of a Greek edition of Athenaeus, whose table talk was so little in demand that no edition in any language appeared in the fifteenth century One trial leaf datable to about 1498 survives to show Aldus's intention, not in the event put into effect until 1514, at the end of his life An ambitious plan for a polyglot Bible was likewise projected and abandoned about this time, as we shall see

The year 1499 brought the death of the patrician backer of the firm, Pierfrancesco Barbarigo. Doubtless Aldus and Torresani took some thought on their future course at this stage in the life of the company, to which in any case the completion of Aristotle in 3700 folio pages had given a natural pause From this time too, small signs appear of pressures on Aldus to change direction Urceo in the letter mentioned above says already in 1498 that he can hope for no favours from Aldus because of 'the greed of his partners' In 1499 Aldus sent his regrets to the secretary of the Florentine republic, Marcello Virgilio Adriani, that he could not offer his books at a discount because they were 'a joint venture with others' The commercial turn things were taking was evident to Janus Lascaris at the end of 1501 when he rebuked Aldus for deserting the printing of Greek books, a desertion motivated solely by the need to make money This is echoed and amplified when in 1505 we hear from one of Aldus's closest coworkers, the Nuremberg Dominican Johannes Cuno, that Torresani was blocking further publication in Greek, something that was independently worrying Aldus's friend Scipione Forteguerri in the same year. The heroic age of Greek printing was past But if survival meant the abandonment of the pure, quixotic vision of a world poring over ancient commentators on Aristotle, it is a measure of Aldus's tenacity that he managed to carry so much of his original programme

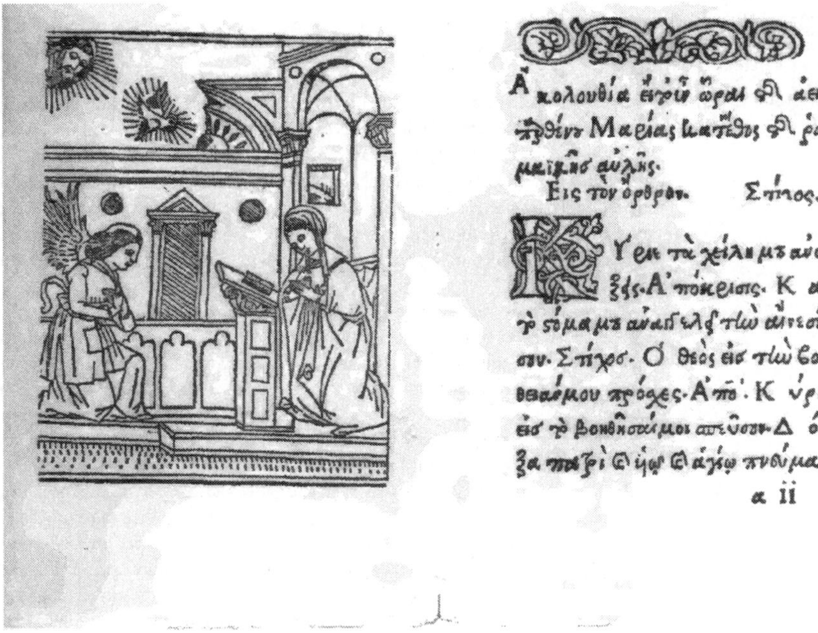

Ἀκολουθία εἰς τὰς ὥρας τῆς ἀειπαρθένου Μαρίας κατὰ ἔθος τῆς ῥωμαϊκῆς αὐλῆς.
Εἰς τὸν ὄρθρον. Στίχος.
Κύριε τὰ χείλη μου ἀνοίξεις. Ἀπόκρισις. Καὶ τὸ στόμα μου ἀναγγελεῖ τὴν αἴνεσίν σου. Στίχος. Ὁ θεὸς εἰς τὴν βοήθειάν μου πρόσχες. Ἀπό. Κύριε εἰς τὸ βοηθῆσαί μοι σπεῦσον. Δόξα πατρὶ καὶ υἱῷ καὶ ἁγίῳ πνεύματι
α ii

nto the sixteenth century against the commercial tide. Retrenchment and ıdaptation were the order of the day.

The change is signalled by two books of 1499 which would have been dis-:inctly out of place in his repertoire till then. In July 1499 he published for the :irst time a work of purely Latin erudition, Niccolò Perotti's *Cornucopiae*. The ɔook was a vast encyclopaedia of the Latin language – more than 700 pages in Aldus's edition – cast in the form of a commentary on part of Martial's epi-grams. This unpromising format had in fact proved extremely popular since its :irst appearance at Venice in 1489, and no fewer than nine editions appeared in :he next decade. It remains to be investigated whether Aldus's assertion that his :dition was superior in having been taken from 'the archetype' is justified. One

13–14
Hypnerotomachia Poliphili, 1499. Two of the triumphal processions which pass by Poliphilo in his dream pursuit of Polia. The excellence of the design – running head, woodcut, massed capitals, woodcut initials and text type – gives a coherence of text and illustration unequalled in incunable printing. The pages show the triumph of Jupiter and Semele (86.k.9, sig. l5) and of Vertumnus and Pomona (IB.24499, sig. m4). Original page-size 304×204 mm (86.k.9) and 286×200 mm (IB.24499).

QVARTVS

LA MVLTITVDINE DEGLI AMANTI GIOVENI, ET DILLE DIVE AMOROSE PVELLE LA NYMPHA APOLIPHILO FACVNDAMENTE DECHIARA, CHI FVRONO ET COME DAGLI DII AMATE. ET GLI CHORI DEGLI DIVI VATICANTANTI, VIDE.

ALCVNO MAI DI TANTO INDEFESSO ELOquio aptamente se accommodarebbe, che gli diuini archani disertando copioso & pienamente potesse euadere & uscire. Et expressamente narrare, & cum quanto di ua pompa, indesinenti Triumphi, perenne gloria, festiua lætitia, & fœlice tripudio, circa a queste quatro iuisitate seiuge de memorando spectamine cum parole sufficientemente exprimere ualesse. Oltra gli inclyti adolescentuli & stipante agmine di inumere & periucunde Nymphe, piu che la tenerecia degli anni sui elle prudente & graue & astutule cum gli acceptissimi amanti de pubescente & depile gene. Ad alcuni la primula lanugine splendescéte le male inserpiua delitiose alacremente festigiauano. Molte hauendo le facole sue accense & ardente. Alcune uidi Pastophore. Altre cum drite haste adornate de prische spolie. Et tali di uarii Trophæi optimaméte ordinate

cum religioso tripudio plaudendo & iubilando, Qualeerano le Nymphe Amadryade, & agli redolenti fiori le Hymenide, riuirente, saliendo iocunde dinanti & da qualũq; lato del floreo Vertunno stricto nella fronte de purpurante & meline rose, cum el gremio pieno de odoriferi & spectatissimi fiori, amanti la stagione del lanoso Ariete, Sedendo ouante sopra una ueterrima Veha, da quatro cornigeri Fauni tirata, Inuinculati de strophie de nouelle fronde, Cum la sua amata & bellissima moglie Pomona coronata de fructi cum ornato defluo degli biõdissimi capigli, parea ello sedẽte, & a gli pedi dellaquale una coctilia Clepsydria iaceua, nel le mane tenente una stipata copia de fiori & maturati fructi cum imixta fogliatura. Præcedẽte la Veha agli trahenti Fauni propinq; due formose Nymphe añsignane, Vna cũ uno hastile Trophæo gerula, de Ligoni. Bidenti. sarculi. & falcionetti, cũ una ꝓpendẽte tabella abaca cũ tale titulo.

INTEGERRIMAM CORPOR. VALITVDINEM, ET STABILE ROBVR, CASTASQVE MEMSAR. DELITIAS, ET BEATAM ANIMI SECVRITATEM CVLTORIB. M. OFFERO.

TIMOKOYPHI
LAPKIA
APTEMEIΣ
ΛΟΝΙ ΧΟ

Excitato ſummopere da tanta ue nuſtate di monumenti indagabondo, ad me uno epigramma alquantulo perplexo candido, in marmoro trouai, ſolamente la parte inſcripta di una arula rimaſta. il reſiduo confracto in terra iaceua.

Cũ maxima delectatione & piacere queſti ſpectandi fragmenti mirando, auido piu anchora indagãte altro di nouo trouare. Dindi dũque qual animale quæritabõdo il pabulo ſem pre piu grato non altramente tranſferendome per gli aggeri di ruine di ingenti fruſti di colũne, & tale integre. Dilleq uale uolendo ſapere la ſorte, una menſuarai al ſolo extẽſa, & dal ſocco fina alla cõtractura, trouai dil ſuo ſcapo la pceritate ſeptẽo diametro dilla ſua ima craſſitudine. Quiui pximo mi ſe offerſe uno ueterrimo ſepulchro, ſencia alcuna ſcriptura, nellaquale per una fractura rimando uidi ſolo le funerale ueſtimenti, & calciamenti petrificati. Coniecturai ragioneuolmente dilla petra ſarcophago (per tale effecto) di troade di Aſia, ſuſpicãdo dil cadauero di Dario.

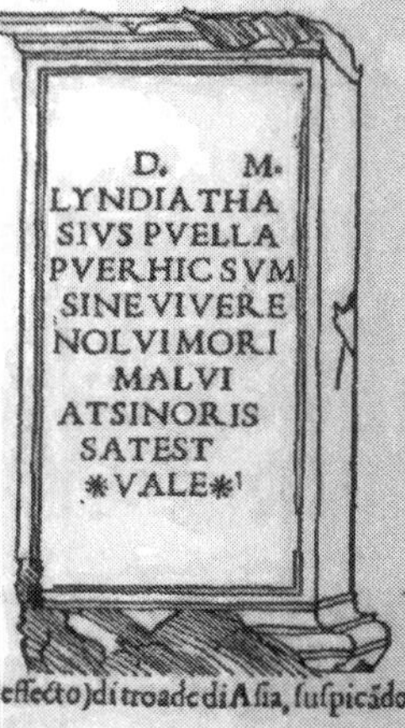
D. M.
LYNDIA THA
SIVS PVELLA
PVER HIC SVM
SINE VIVERE
NOLVI MORI
MALVI
AT SI NORIS
SAT EST
VALE[1]

Et ad uicino uidi uno nobile ſepulchro di porphyrite, exquiſitamente excalpto tra ſiluatichi arbuſcoli, dilquale mi ſe offerſe ad legere uno elegante epitaphio, & hauea il coopertorio in templo egregio, & ſcandulato ſquameamente, una parte dil dicto ſopra larca riſtato, & laltra iaceua deiecta ſoliſtima, & di tale præſtante titulo inſcripto.

real and useful innovation (with a remote German precedent) was the first appearance of pagination in an Italian printed book, half-leaves (as Aldus called them) equipped with 'arithmeticis numeris'. In conjunction with the lineation supplied for easy reference, this procedure transferred to the printer the work Aldus had instructed the reader to perform for himself in the preface to the 1497 Greek-Latin dictionary.

15
Romantic archaeology in the *Hypnerotomachia*: Poliphilo and his beloved Polia find themselves in a cemetery full of inscriptions commemorating lovers who had died for love. Original page-size 304×204 mm. 86.k.9, sig. q6ᵛ.

Very different again was the *Hypnerotomachia Poliphili*, the first vernacular text printed by Aldus (Figs 13 - 15, 17). It is nowadays the most celebrated of his editions, and the most controversial. The fame of the book arises from its magnificent woodcuts, the controversy attends the authorship of both the woodcuts and the text. The *Hypnerotomachia* is a prose romance in two books which narrates the symbolic dream of Poliphilo and the story of his love for Polia, a lady of Treviso. The whole story is cast as the 'strife of love in a dream', as the title translates, and is shot through with a dreamlike mix of allegory, archaeology and myth. It draws both upon the earlier antiquarianism of the humanists Ciriaco d'Ancona and Felice Feliciano and upon the current fashion for difficult and technical late Latin prose. That fashion is here transmuted into an extraordinarily exotic Latinate vernacular, a language never spoken and never again attempted in Italian literature.

The question of authorship has been hotly debated in recent years. The old theory - dating back to the early sixteenth century - which ascribes it to Fra Francesco Colonna on the basis of an acrostic picked out of the beautiful woodcut capitals that begin each chapter, and confirmed by an initial printed poem in a single copy in Berlin, seems still to be the most likely. Fra Francesco was a priest and novice master at Treviso who became a decidedly unreformed sort of Dominican at the Venetian house of SS. Giovanni e Paolo. We know a good deal about his career, chiefly from documents of the many legal cases in which his wayward lifestyle embroiled him. One of these documents demands from him (in 1501) the return of a loan made by the Dominicans for help in printing the book. Yet the main subvention for the printing costs came from Leonardus Crassus (Leonardo Grassi, papal protonotary, a friend of the late Ermolao Barbaro), whose letter of dedication to the Duke of Urbino mentions that he has had the edition printed at his own expense. And indeed a decade later the record shows Grassi seeking an extension for a further ten years of the privilege which protected the book in Venetian territory. The *Hypnerotomachia*, into which he had sunk 'several hundred ducats', had failed to sell in the disturbed state of Italy at the time, riven by war and plague as it was - and an Italian text could find no market outside Italy.

The failure surprises us, but perhaps it did not greatly surprise Aldus. The book provides the first clear example in his output of commissioned work,

16
Pietro Bembo, *De Aetna*, 1496 This dialogue between Pietro Bembo and his father Bernardo was Aldus's first publication wholly in Latin A new roman typeface was designed for it, derivatives of which still bear Bembo's name Original page-size 196×149 mm
G 9289, sig A2v

explicabo; non tanq̃ recenſeatur. Igitur; cum illum multa in umbra ſedentem
compériſſem; ita initium interpellandi
eum feci. PETRVS BEMBVS FILI
VS. Diu quidem pâter hic ſedes: & certe
ripa haec uirens; quam populi tuae iſtae
denſiſſimae inumbrant; & fluuius alit; ali
quanto frigidior eſt fortaſſe, q̃ ſit ſatis.
BERNARDVS BEMBVS PATER.
Ego uero fili nuſpiam eſſe libentius ſoleo;
q̃ in hac cum ripae, tum arborum, tum
etiam fluminis amoenitate: neq; eſt, quod
uereare, nequid nobis frigus hoc noceat,
praeſertim in tanto aeſtatis ardore: Sed
feciſti tu quidem pérbene; qui me ab iis
cogitationibus reuocaſti; quas & libentiſ-
ſime ſemper abiicio, cum in Nonianum
uenitur; et nũc quidem nobis neſcio quo
pacto furtim irrepſerant non modo non
uocantibus, ſed etiam inuitis.
BEMBVS FILIVS. De rep. ſci
licet cogitabas aliquid, aut certe de trium

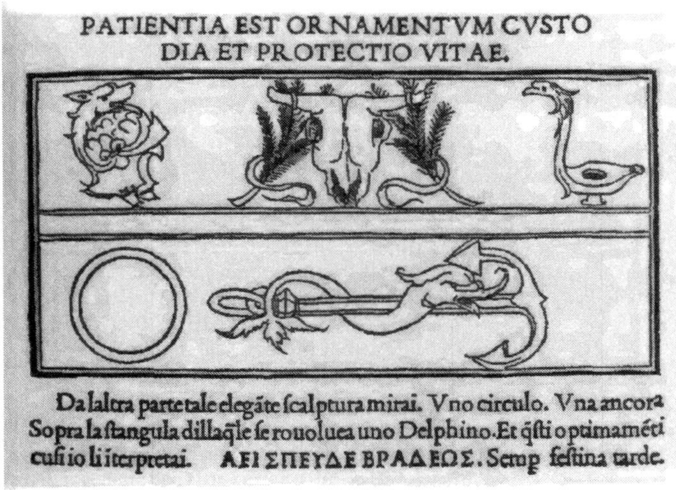

PATIENTIA EST ORNAMENTVM CVSTO
DIA ET PROTECTIO VITAE.
Da laltra parte tale elegãte ſcalptura mirai. Vno circulo. Vna ancora
Sopra la ſtangula dilla q̃le ſe rouolueua uno Delphino. Et q̃ſti optimamẽti
cuſi io li iterpretai. ΑΕΙ ΣΠΕΥΔΕ ΒΡΑΔΕΩΣ. Semp feſtina tarde.

17
The significance of symbols: the first appearance of the dolphin and anchor in Aldine work (*Hypnerotomachia* sig. d7), later adopted as Aldus's printer's device. The text offers the interpretation in Latin and Greek: 'hasten slowly'.
Detail of IB.24499.

undertaken entirely at the risk of outside backers. His part in the printing is confined to an unemphatic colophon at the end of an *errata* list, the preface and commendatory verses being left to those responsible for the publication. Yet Aldus cannot have failed to take a close interest in the setting up of the romance, for it demanded and got the very highest standard of book production. The Aldine roman, first cut by Griffo for Bembo's *Aetna* in 1496 (Fig.16) and recut with a larger and lighter upper case in 1499, is justly famous for its clarity and beauty; in the words of George Painter, it was the first fifteenth-century type 'consciously designed according to purely typographical ideals, in liberation from manuscript models'. The 'Bembo' type is here sometimes laid out so as to represent the objects described in the text, in the ancient tradition of *technopaignia*.

The great distinction of the *Hypnerotomachia*, however, lies in its blending of type, woodcut capitals and woodcut illustrations in a harmonious whole. The illustrations themselves closely follow the text as Poliphilo moves through the dream landscape of ancient ruins and shattered inscriptions, arcane hieroglyphs and obelisks, triumphal processions of nymphs and satyrs. The great beauty of the classicizing style of these woodcuts has provoked many attempts to identify the artist with a known master, none of which has met with widespread favour. Part of the difficulty lies in matching a painter or illuminator's style to

18
Epistole of St Catherine of Siena, 1500 The hand of the artist of the *Hypnerotomachia* has been seen in the fine woodcut which faces the beginning of the text
St Catherine holds a book inscribed with the very first italic type
Original page-size 308×210 mm
IB 24504, sig [*]10^{v}

what appears in the coarser medium of woodblocks, generally cut by a workman from a master's design. The most that can be said with assurance is that the designer was familiar with the work of Andrea Mantegna and Giovanni Bellini, and lies within that ambit of north Italian classicism which contributed so much to the hand-painted illumination of incunabula (see Frontispiece) We have no information on the relations of Aldus with anyone connected with the commission, nor with the artist of the woodcuts But the printed mis-en-page is so carefully arranged that it is impossible to think that he did not have direct dealings with the author and illustrator. At the very least the dolphin and anchor on fol d7 (Fig 17), one of the many representations of 'hasten slowly' in the book, seized Aldus's imagination, becoming in due course his motto and his printer's device.

Commissioned work continued in 1500 with the production of another edition outside the 'programmatic' range of Aldine texts The Italian *Letters* of St Catharine of Siena were printed in September 1500 on behalf of Margherita Ugelheimer (Fig 18) She was the Venetian widow of the German partner of Nicholas Jenson, a man of great wealth if we may judge from the supreme quality of the artists he engaged to add painted illumination to his incunables Thanks to a surviving agreement written in Aldus's hand we know that manuscripts of the *Letters* were sought from a Dominican monastery in Venice and taken for printing against a sum of sixty ducats should they be damaged, the monastery was also to receive ten copies of the printed book in exchange for the loan The text, though quite different from the character of Aldine production hitherto, was by no means alien to Aldus's deep religiosity, to which he gave full expression in a letter of dedication to the future Pius III.

A NEW STYLE OCTAVO AND ITALIC

The times were very uncertain. Venetian defeats and Turkish advances caused the collapse of the long credit printers needed, and many firms went to the wall in the period around 1500 The business of Aldus and Torresani was one of the fortunate survivors, and actually began to thrive against a background of general economic gloom. But this was accomplished only by setting out on a new path Several factors must have come together in the partners' minds

We have seen the gradual abandonment of exclusive reliance on Greek editions, for the most part of an increasingly recherché nature. Works such as the Perotti and St Catharine showed the way to ready sales of Latin and vernacular texts. The only other edition Aldus issued in 1500 was a quarto Lucretius Unlike most major Latin poets, Lucretius had not at that point attracted any humanist commentary His plain text in the Aldine makes a striking contrast to

TRANSIIT AD SPONSVM TRIBVS EXORNATA CORONIS

19
Lucretius, *De rerum natura*, 1500 A plain text, using the initials of the *Hypnerotomachia* and edited for Aldus by the humanist Girolamo Avanzi Original page-size 211×152 mm
G 9474, sig a1

the sea of commentary that washed against small islands of text in late fifteenth-century Venetian editions of the poets (Fig.19) There was at the same time a move in the world of luxury manuscript production towards small-format codices of the Latin classics, portable, often highly decorated, stripped of the apparatus of scholarship that tradition dictated in didactic contexts

The precise origins of the Aldine italic pocket-books are still a matter of debate It is certain, however, that Aldus was well acquainted with such small manuscripts of poetic texts. He comes close to saying, in dedicatory remarks addressed to Pietro Bembo in his 1514 edition of Virgil, that books in the possession of Pietro's father, Bernardo, had given him the idea of the format for the octavo series which is one of his great innovations The innovation lay not in the small format, often used by printers for devotional texts, but in applying it to a class of literature hitherto issued in large and imposing folios or quartos It is also certain that the small-format manuscripts in Bernardo Bembo's library included a good number written by the leading Paduan scribe, Bartolomeo Sanvito, whose hand seems to be the best and closest model for the Aldine italic

This famous type was a sympathetic rendering by Francesco Griffo of the best humanist cursive script of the day, a wholly new departure in Latin typography but parallel to Aldus's adaptation of Greek cursive hands for his earlier work. If italic has today become practically confined to words that convention dictates be 'italicized', we must also recognize that it appeared to contemporaries as a revelation of elegance – to Erasmus, 'the neatest types in the world' The narrow set of the type is also very economical of paper, an important consideration in those days The very first appearance is in a few words set in the woodcut that adorns the folio St Catherine (Fig 18), followed by limited use in the preface to the second (quarto) edition of Aldus's Latin grammar of February 1501 Italic reached its manifest destiny as the text type of the book which began Aldus's great series of octavo classics, the Virgil of April 1501 (Figs 20-21) True to the aspirations of the series, the preface is one of the briefest of any Aldine edition· 'this purified text is offered in the form in which you see it, the minor and obscene poems we have not thought worth putting in this handbook (*enchiridium*) It is our intention to print all the best authors in this same type '

The aims of the *enchiridia* are more illuminatingly put in the preface to Horace, addressed in May to Aldus's old friend, the patrician diarist Marin Sanudo (who had also received the dedication of the 1498 Politian) The emphasis is placed on the inviting smallness of the book, which could supply reading matter for the odd moments snatched from Sanudo's labours on behalf of the republic Here lies the key to the octavos and their market. The editions were not designed, like the vast folios of Aristotle and their fellows, for the high-level humanist scholar and university professional. They were, as Aldus put it in the

.T.LVCRETII CARI DE RERVM NATVRA, LIBER PRIMVS.

AEneadum genitrix homi-
num, diuum' que uoluptas
alma Venus, cæli subter la
bentia signa
quæ mare nauigerum, quæ
terras frugiferenteis
concelebras, per te quoni
am genus omne animantum
concipitur, uisit' que exortum lumina Solis,
te Dea te fugiunt uenti, te nubila cæli,
aduentum' que tuum, tibi suaueis dædala tellus
submittit flores, tibi rident æquora ponti,
placatum' que nitet diffuso numine cælum.
Nam simulac species patefactast uerna diei,
et reserata uiget genitabilis aura fauonii,
aeriæ primum uolucres te diua, tuum' que
significant initum perculsæ corda tua ui.
Inde feræ pecudes persu ltant pabula læta,
et rapidos tranant amneis, ita capta lepore
te sequitur cupide, quo quanque inducere pergis.
Denique per maria, ac monteis, fluuios' que rapaceis,
frondiferas' que domos auium, campos' que uirenteis
omnibus incutiens blandum per pectora amorem
efficis, ut cupide generatim secla propagent.
Quæ quoniam rerum naturam sola gubernas,
nec sine te quicquam dias in luminis oras
exoritur, neq; fit lætum, neque amabile quicquam,
te sociam studeo scribendis uersibus esse,
quos ego de rerum natura pangere conor
Memmiadæ nostro, quem tu dea tempore in omni,
omnibus ornatum uoluisti excellere rebus.
Quo magis æternum da dictis diua leporem,

a.

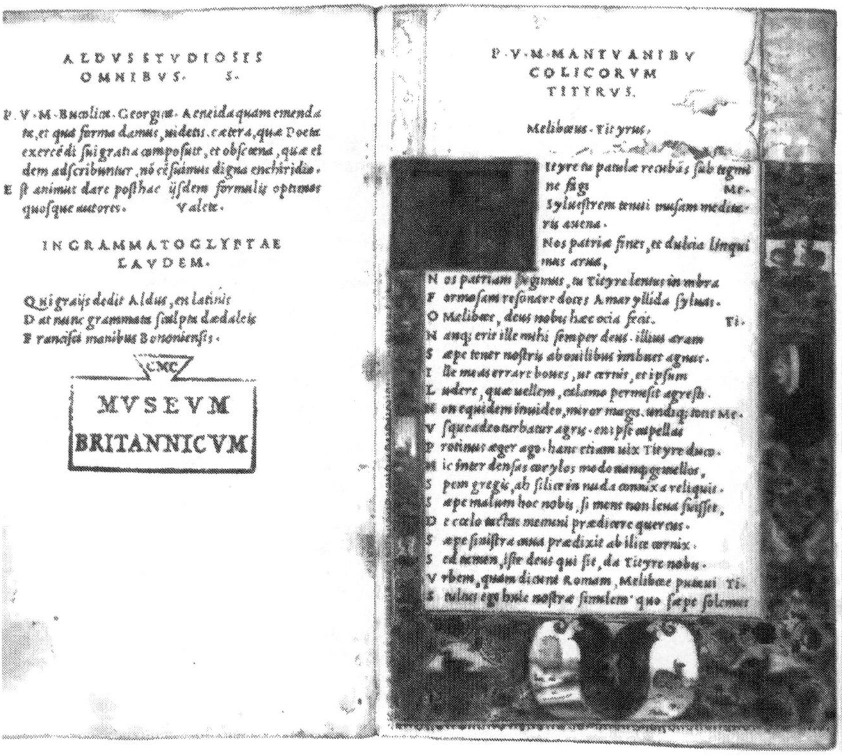

ALDVS STVDIOSIS
OMNIBVS. S.

P. V. M. Bucolica. Georgica. Aeneida quam emendata, et qua forma damus, uidetis. caetera, quae Poetae exercendi sui gratia composuit, et obscoena, quae eidem adscribuntur, nō cēsuimus digna enchiridio. Est animus dare posthac iisdem formulis optimos quosque autores. Valete.

IN GRAMMATOGLYPTAE
LAVDEM.

Qui graiis dedit Aldus, en latinis
Dat nunc grammata scalpta daedaleis
Francisci manibus Bononiensis.

P. V. M. MANTVANI BV
COLICORVM
TITYRVS.

Meliboeus. Tityrus.

Tityre tu patulae recubās sub tegmine fagi Me.
Syluestrem tenui musam meditaris auena.
Nos patriae fines, et dulcia linquimus arua,
Nos patriam fugimus, tu Tityre lentus in umbra
Formosam resonare doces Amaryllida syluas.
O Meliboee, deus nobis haec ocia fecit. Ti.
Namq; erit ille mihi semper deus. illius aram
Saepe tener nostris ab ouilibus imbuet agnus.
Ille meas errare boues, ut cernis, et ipsum
Ludere, quae uellem, calamo permisit agresti.
Non equidem inuideo, miror magis. undiq; totis Me.
Vsque adeo turbatur agris. en ipse capellas
Protinus aeger ago. hanc etiam uix Tityre duco.
Hic inter densas corylos modo nanq; gemellos,
Spem gregis, ah silice in nuda connixa reliquit.
Saepe malum hoc nobis, si mens non laeua fuisset,
De coelo tactas memini praedicere quercus.
Saepe sinistra caua praedixit ab ilice cornix.
Sed tamen, iste deus qui sit, da Tityre nobis.
Vrbem, quam dicunt Romam, Meliboee putaui Ti.
Stultus ego huic nostrae similem quo saepe solemus

20
Opera of Virgil, 1501. The first of the octavo classics, and the first book printed wholly in italic type. Aldus pays tribute to Francesco Griffo, the designer of the type, in the verses on the left-hand page. Original page-size 154×87 mm.
C.19.f.7, sig. a1ᵛ–a2.

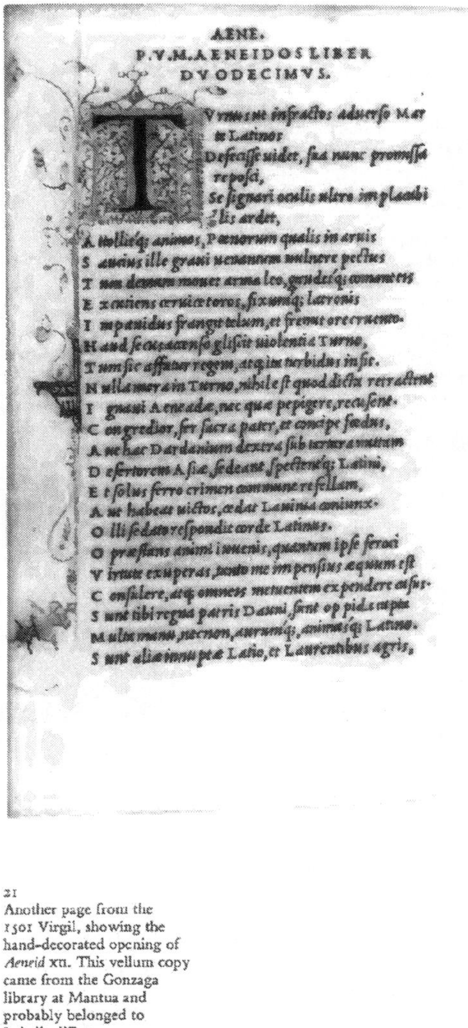
AENE.
P.V.M.AENEIDOS LIBER
DVODECIMVS.
Vrnus ut infractos aduerso Mar
te Latinos
Defecisse uidet, sua nunc promissa
reposci,
Se signari oculis ultro implacabi
lis ardet,
A ttollitq; animos, Poenorum qualis in aruis
S aucius ille graui uenantum uulnere pectus
T um demum mouet arma leo, gaudetq; comantes
E xcutiens ceruice toros, fixumq; latronis
I mpauidus frangit telum, et fremit ore cruento.
H aud secus accenso gliscit uiolentia Turno,
T um sic affatur regem, atq; ita turbidus infit.
N ulla mora in Turno, nihil est quod dicta retractent
I gnaui Aeneadae, nec quae pepigere, recusent.
C ongredior, fer sacra pater, et concipe foedus,
A ut hac Dardanium dextra sub tartara mittam
D esertorem Asiae, sedeant spectentq; Latini,
E t solus ferro crimen commune refellam,
A ut habeat uictos, cedat Lauinia coniunx.
O lli sedato respondit corde Latinus.
O praestans animi iuuenis, quantum ipse feroci
V irtute exuperas, tanto me impensius aequum est
C onsulere, atq; omnes metuentem expendere casus.
S unt tibi regna patris Dauni, sunt oppida capta
M ulta manu, nec non aurumq; animusq; Latino.
S unt aliae innuptae Latio, et Laurentibus agris,

21
Another page from the 1501 Virgil, showing the hand-decorated opening of *Aeneid* XII. This vellum copy came from the Gonzaga library at Mantua and probably belonged to Isabella d'Este.
Actual size.
C.19.f.7, sig. v2v.

22
Gli Asolani of Pietro Bembo, a vernacular dialogue on the nature of love printed in 1505 The end of the text is followed by the colophon and one of Aldus's frequent notices of privilege, protecting the work against reprinting by others within the Venetian dominion for a period of ten years Original page-size 204×123 mm
G 10472, sig m8

second of his advertisements, dated 1503, 'libelli portatiles', books which could be carried about – and read – by persons who had education but little leisure, or education and too much leisure. in other words, politicians and diplomats and officers of state, prelates of the church and cultivated members of the rich Italian courts The setting at the court of Asolo of Bembo's dialogue *Gli Asolani* (published by Aldus in 1505 Fig 22) and at the court of Urbino of Castiglione's *Il Cortegiano* (printed by Aldus's heirs in 1528) exactly catches the refined world which he was now penetrating books for ladies and gentlemen Many of these were poetic texts where the massed italic was less apt to weary the eye than long lines of prose

And *these* books sold By the time of the dedication to Bembo in 1514, Aldus had already exhausted two editions of the works of Virgil (which we can estimate to have been about 3000 for each run). By contrast, nearly all the incunable editions of his Greek folios were still available in the third advertisement of 1513, some at reduced prices Not that the octavos were cheap – Isabella d'Este, the learned Marchioness of Mantua (and another former pupil of Battista Guarino), sent back some vellum copies she had ordered when she was told by her courtiers that they were worth no more than half the price Aldus's partners were asking These may have been special illuminated copies costing five ducats or more – some exquisite vellum editions that she did buy from Aldus survive in the British Library – but even the plain paper copies, according to Aldus's annotation of the 1503 advertisement, went for a substantial quarter of a ducat.

The octavos of the amazingly productive years from 1501 to 1505 embraced classics of Italian as well as Latin literature, notably the poems of Petrarch and Dante (Figs 23 - 24), both of them printed with the funds and manuscripts of Pietro Bembo and his brother Carlo These two editions marked a radical overhaul and purification of the text of the Tuscan poets They were to prove of central importance for the development of Italian vernacular literature in the sixteenth century, in which Pietro Bembo took a leading part There was even a small octavo selection of the major Greek authors such as Homer (Fig 25) and the tragedians, set in the last, smallest and clearest of the four Aldine greeks Here again editorial and typographical labour, not to speak of the limited sale such works could expect, exacted a price. The Greek authors are typically offered at two or three times what a Latin book of comparable extent would fetch

For the steadiest Latin sellers the Aldines soon had competition from counterfeiters in Italy, and more especially in France The printers of Lyons became rapidly expert in reproducing the italic types and exact texts of their models, even down to Aldus's own prefaces. Aldus took extensive precautions, securing

mossi, ritornare; et aperti quegliocchi, che in questo ca mino si chiudono, mirare con essi quella ineffabile bellezza, di cui sono amante sua dolce merce gia buon tempo: et hora perche io uecchio sia, come tu mi uedi; ella non m'ha percio meno, che in altra eta, caro: ne mi risiutera; perche io di cosi grosso panno uestito le uada innanzi. Quantunque ne io con questo panno u'andro; ne tu con quello u'andrai: ne altro di questi luoghi si porta alcuno seco dipartendosi, che gli suoi amori: Equali se sono stati di queste bellezze, che qua giu sono; percio che esse cola su non sagliono, ma rimangono alla terra di cui sono figliuole; essi ci tormentano; si come hora ci sogliono quegli disii tormentare, dequali godere non si puo ne molto ne poco: Se sono di quelle di la su stati; essi marauigliosamente ci trastullano, poscia che ad esse peruenuti pienamente ne godiamo. Ma percio che quella dimora è sempiterna; si dee credere Lauinello, che buono Amore sia quello, delquale godere si puo eternamente; et reo quell'altro, che eternamente ci condanna a dolere. Queste cose ragionatemi dal santo huomo; percio che tempo era, che io mi dipartissi; esso mi licentiò. Ilche poscia che hebbe detto Lauinello; a suoi ragionamenti pose fine.

I mpressi in Venetia nelle Case d'Aldo Romano nel anno . M D V . del mese di Marzo; Con la concessione della Illustrissima Signoria nostra; che per . x . anni ne luoghi al Venetiano Domino sottoposti nessuno altro gli possa imprimere, o impressi uendere, sotto le pene, che in lei si contengono.

23
Francesco Petrarca, *Opere volgari*, 1501. This vellum copy of Petrarch's Italian poetry, edited by Pietro Bembo from the autograph manuscript, was illuminated for Isabella d'Este, a frequent purchaser of Aldine octavo editions. Actual size.
C.20.b.29, sig. a2.

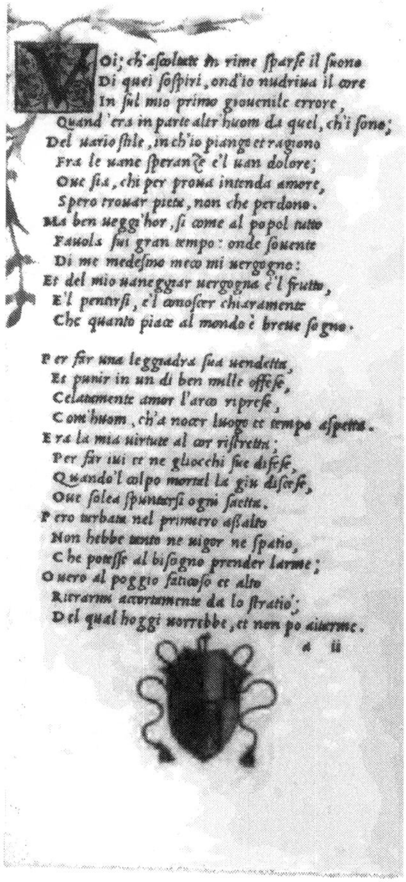
Voi; ch'ascoltate in rime sparse il suono
Di quei sospiri, ond'io nudriua il core
In sul mio primo giouenile errore,
Quand'era in parte altr'huom da quel, ch'i sono;
Del uario stile, in ch'io piango et ragiono
Fra le uane speranze e'l uan dolore;
Oue sia, chi per proua intenda amore,
Spero trouar pieta, non che perdono.
Ma ben ueggi'hor, si come al popol tutto
Fauola fui gran tempo: onde souente
Di me medesmo meco mi uergogno:
Et del mio uaneggiar uergogna e'l frutto,
E'l pentirsi, e'l conoscer chiaramente
Che quanto piace al mondo è breue sogno.

Per far una leggiadra sua uendetta,
Et punir in un di ben mille offese,
Celatamente amor l'arco riprese,
Com'huom, ch'a nocer luogo et tempo aspetta.
Era la mia uirtute al cor ristretta;
Per far iui et ne gliocchi sue difese,
Quando'l colpo mortal la giu discese,
Oue solea spuntarsi ogni saetta.
Pero turbata nel primiero assalto
Non hebbe tanto ne uigor ne spatio,
Che potesse al bisogno prender l'arme;
Ouero al poggio faticoso et alto
Ritrarmi accortamente da lo stratio;
Del qual hoggi uorrebbe, et non po aitarme.
a ii

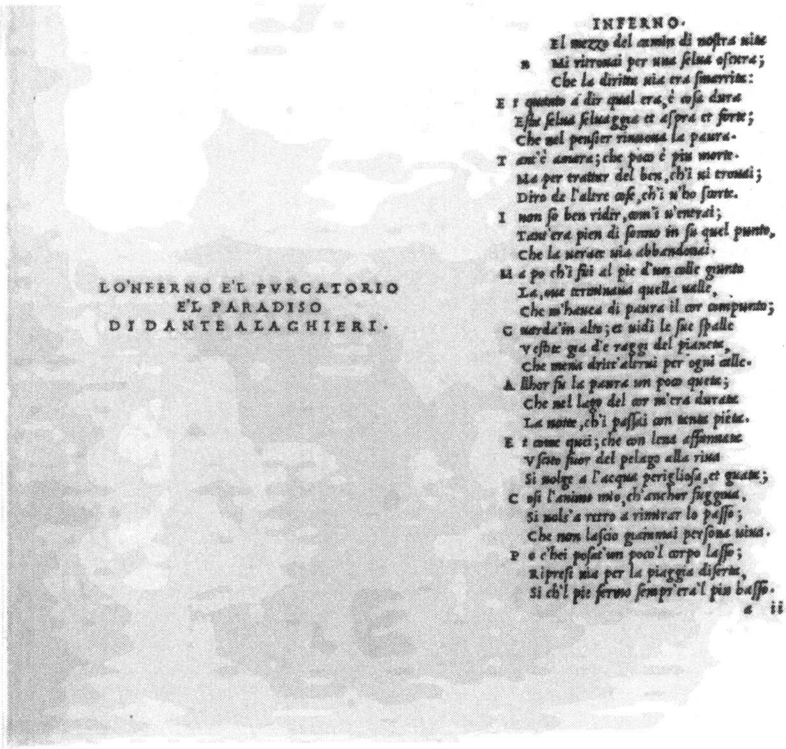

LO'NFERNO E'L PVRGATORIO
E'L PARADISO
DI DANTE ALAGHIERI.

INFERNO.

N El mezzo del camin di nostra uita
Mi ritrouai per una selua oscura;
Che la diritta uia era smarrita:
E t quanto a dir qual era, è cosa dura
Esta selua seluaggia et aspra et forte;
Che nel pensier rinnoua la paura.
T ant'è amara; che poco è piu morte.
Ma per trattar del ben, ch'i ui trouai;
Dirò de l'altre cose, ch'i u'ho scorte.
I non so ben ridir, com'i u'entrai;
Tant'era pien di sonno in su quel punto,
Che la uerace uia abbandonai.
M a po ch'i fui al pie d'un colle giunto
La, oue terminaua quella ualle,
Che m'hauea di paura il cor compunto;
G uardai in alto; et uidi le sue spalle
Vestite gia de raggi del pianeta,
Che mena dritt'altrui per ogni calle.
A llhor fu la paura un poco queta;
Che nel lago del cor m'era durata
La notte, ch'i passai con tanta pieta.
E t come quei; che con lena affannata
Vscito fuor del pelago alla riua
Si uolge a l'acqua perigliosa, et guata;
C osi l'animo mio, ch'ancho fuggiua,
Si uols'a retro a rimirar lo passo;
Che non lasciò giamai persona uiua.
P oi c'hei posat'un poco'l corpo lasso;
Ripresi uia per la piaggia diserta,
Si ch'l pie fermo sempr'era'l piu basso.

a ii

24
Dante, *Comedia*, 1502. Like the Petrarch of the year before, this edition presented a bare, uncommented text (unusual for Dante's works) edited by Pietro Bembo. This soon displaced all others as the vulgate text of Italy's greatest poet. Original page-size 164×96 mm. 679.a.18, sig. a1^{v}–a2.

in 1501 - 02 Venetian privileges and papal bulls to protect not only individual titles but his entire italic design It was all to no avail In exasperation he issued a remarkable broadsheet, the *Monitum* or 'warning' of 16 March 1503, which specified exactly what readers had to look for if they wanted the genuine Aldine article. The textual shortcomings of the Lyonnese editions are given in detail, signed off with the proud flourish of Aldus's dolphin and anchor device, which he had employed since 1501. The Lyons printers, who never precisely claimed to be producing Aldines, went on printing in the 'Aldine' italic for the rest of his life and beyond, cheerfully aware of the ineffectiveness of privileges, bulls and warnings from the south

GREEK SCHOLARSHIP AND HEBREW AMBITIONS

The counterfeits must have had some damaging effect on the sale of the Venetian *enchiridia*, but the genuine products all the same kept the firm of Aldus and Torresani buoyant, acting as a cross-subsidy for less remunerative publications For Aldus did not turn his back on the sort of publishing that had first gained him a reputation, and the first years of the sixteenth century yielded a good crop of scholarly *editiones principes*, as usual issued in folio The two major Greek historians, Herodotus and Thucydides, known in the West only in the Renaissance Latin translations of Lorenzo Valla, were both issued in the original language in 1502 (Fig 26) The Ammonius of 1502 and the Philoponus of 1504, followed at some distance by Alexander of Aphrodisias in 1513, at last began to make good the promise made in 1495 to equip Aristotle with his ancient commentators Like all the Aristotelian works, these volumes are dedicated to Aldus's old and still steady supporter Alberto Pio, in compliment to whom Aldus added Pius to his own name in 1503. The first editions of Demosthenes (1504), the huge *Moralia* of Plutarch (1509, Fig.27), and the two-part collection of Greek rhetoricians which straddled the years 1508 and 1509 all continued the work, as the editor of the last, Demetrius Ducas, remarked in the preface, of shoring up Greek prose literature against extinction The *Rhetorica graeca* included two vital Aristotelian works omitted from the incunable Aristotle, the *Rhetoric* and the *Poetics*. Aldus even rescued from long obscurity the works of the ancient Christian Latin poets (1502) and the Greek poems, with Latin translation, of the Church Father Gregory of Nazianzen (1504) Both these editions, expressly designed for the education of Christian youth, suffered long delays in the printing office due to the difficulty of securing texts and translations, besides unspecified problems that Aldus had with his workmen

One emblematic case may illustrate Aldus's scholarly plans, and the extent to which they fell short of execution. The first use of Hebrew type in Venice

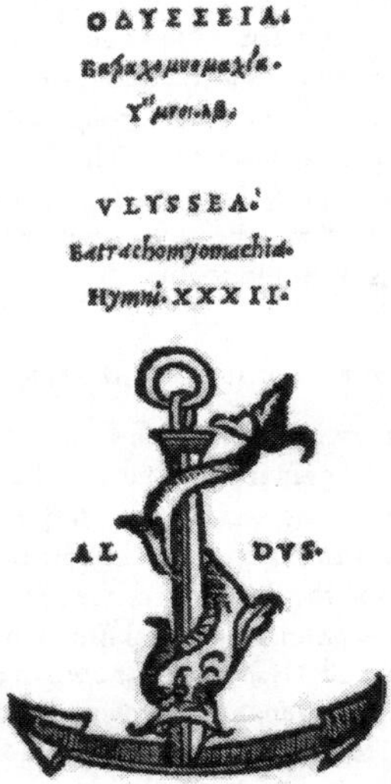
ΟΔΥΣΣΕΙΑ.
Βατραχομυομαχία.
Ὕμνοι. λβ.

VLYSSEA.
Batrachomyomachia.
Hymni. XXXII.

AL DVS.

25
Homer, *Odyssey*, etc. Aldus issued Homer's *Iliad* and *Odyssey* in October 1504, a select Greek addition to the octavo classics.
Actual size.
G.8722, fol. 1.

26
Herodotus, 1502 With this book and the Thucydides of the same year, Aldus gave the world the first editions in the original language of the two major historians of classical Greece This page shows Greek annotations made by Erasmus in his own copy Original page-size 306×205 mm
C 45 k 6, sig 4A2

(though Jewish printers had been printing whole books in Hebrew elsewhere since about 1470) occurs in the Politian, *Opera* of 1498. A few words there, quoted to explain a philological point, may well have been cut specially by Francesco Griffo, like the sporadic phrases in the same Hebrew characters in the *Hypnerotomachia* of 1499 As early as 1498 something much more ambitious was in the air Aldus permitted both Justin Decadyus, editor of the Greek Psalter in that year, and William Grocyn, his English helper with the ancient astronomical texts of 1499, to record in print that he was proposing to publish the Holy Scriptures in a trilingual edition of Greek, Latin and Hebrew. How he came by his interest in Hebrew we do not know but his home town in distant Bassiano had an ancient Jewish community, and his friends Giovanni Pico and Johann Reuchlin were in the vanguard of the Christian study of the language as part of the indivisible heritage of antiquity Reuchlin indeed, an author Aldus had printed in 1498, later addressed him as learned in all three ancient languages, and he if anyone, the leading Hebraist of the day, was in a position to know

All that remains of the trilingual Bible is a pair of proof sheets in Paris with the opening of Genesis in two different settings and three columns of type, the first an entirely new, and very beautiful, square Hebrew with pointing for vowels (Fig 28) Another German friend, Conrad Celtes, was apparently sent such specimens in September 1501, but by August 1502 Aldus had to report to Reuchlin that nothing in Hebrew had been printed This particular return *ad fontes* lapsed at this point It was without precedent but not without sequel, the idea being taken up again in a few years in the Polyglot Psalter at Paris and the great Polyglot Bible of Alcalá, the latter was helped in its long gestation (1514-22) by Greek editorial work of Aldus's own editor Demetrius Ducas.

The trilingual Bible was stillborn, but there exists an intriguing offshoot, a little introduction to learning Hebrew The *Introductio utilissima hebraice discere cupientibus* is constructed very much along the lines of the *Brevissima introductio* to Greek of about 1497. an alphabet in the handsome Bible type is followed by the combinations of Hebrew letters and some very brief and simple biblical reading matter, the whole with Latin pronunciations and translation As so often with the Greek books, Aldus promises much more – grammars, dictionaries, sacred texts – if this modest venture should find a welcome with the public In its presumed original form of about 1500 it survives as a unique copy at the John Rylands University Library in Manchester, a miniature 16° book printed in black and red (Fig 29) It was soon added as supplementary material to other grammars – to Constantine Lascaris's *Erotemata*, and to Aldus's own Latin grammar, both of which were re-issued about 1501, and many later editions by Aldus and others The old urge to instruct never left him.

Aldus does not explicitly put forward the Hebrew *Introductio* as his own

ΗΡΟΔΟΤΟΥ ΑΛΙΚΑΡΝΑΣΣΕΩΣ ΙΣΤΟΡΙΑ ΕΝ ΕΝΝΕΑ ΤΜΗΜΑΣΙΝ, Α ΚΑΙ ΜΟΥΣΑΣ ΚΑΛΕΙ. ΙΣΤΟΡΙΩΝ ΠΡΩΤΗ. ΚΛΕΙΩ.

[illegible]

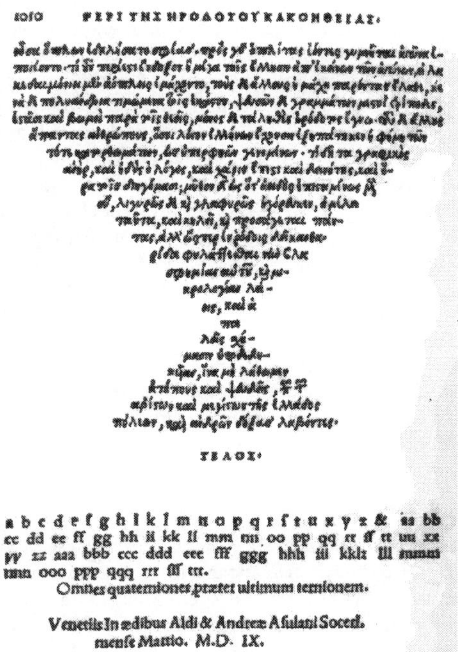

1010 ΠΕΡΙ ΤΗΣ ΗΡΟΔΟΤΟΥ ΚΑΚΟΗΘΕΙΑΣ.

[illegible]

ΤΕΛΟΣ.

a b c d e f g h i k l m n o p q r f t u x y z & aa bb cc dd ee ff gg hh ii kk ll mm nn oo pp qq rr ff tt uu xx yy zz aaa bbb ccc ddd eee fff ggg hhh iii kkk lll mmm nnn ooo ppp qqq rrr fff ttt.

Omnes quaterniones, præter ultimum ternionem.

Venetiis In ædibus Aldi & Andreæ Afulani Soceri. menfe Martio. M.D. IX.

work, and in fact in 1510 the famous Jewish printer Gershom Soncino laid violent claim to it as his own youthful composition which someone (understand, Aldus) had corruptly printed. It was this same Soncino who in dedicating his 1503 italic Petrarch mentioned that he had obtained the services of the famous punchcutter Messer Francesco da Bologna, who had cut all the types that Aldus ever printed with. Both Soncino (who seems to have been excluded from Venetian territory by legal action of Aldus) and Griffo (who himself took credit for the success of the 'Aldine' italic in yet another Petrarch, in 1516) nursed grudges against Aldus over long years. Yet Aldus never involved himself in polemic, nor suffered others to publish polemical works from his press (difficult, in those days). His rupture with Griffo is signalled by no more than the removal from later editions of the delicate three-line tribute with which he had introduced his italic punchcutter in the first octavo book, the Virgil of 1501 (Fig.20). The superb hebrew type remains, along with the fourth Aldine greek, as Griffo's last great creation for Aldus. As for Hebrew publication, those dreams too stayed with him. Near the end of his life, in the 1513 Pindar, he was still proclaiming his intention to print in the original language the books which, translated from Hebrew into Greek and thence into Latin, had become the sacred core of the Judaeo-Christian tradition.

27
Plutarch, *Moralia*. The last page with patterned text, quire register (to tell the owner or binder the full complement of gatherings), and colophon: 'Printed at Venice in the house of Aldus and his father-in-law Andrea of Asola, March 1509'. Original page-size 290×188 mm. C.8149, p.1050.

THE ACADEMY AND ERASMUS

The reasons for the failure of so many announced projects must be sought in a complex interaction of personal inclinations and discouragement, pressures from friends and the needs of commerce, and more generally the larger external pressures brought to bear by political upheaval and war. The story of the Aldine New Academy is witness to all of these. It seems that from quite early in the sixteenth century Aldus nourished an ambition to create a formal learned society in imitation of the ancient Academy of Plato, and recalling the 'academies' that had gathered around Bessarion in Rome and Lorenzo de' Medici in Florence. From 1502 books were issued with the words 'ex neacademia nostra' in the colophon. There exists a single printed sheet in the Vatican Library which sets out the rules for meetings of this Academy (Fig.30). The text is entirely in the Greek of one of Aldus's long-standing colleagues, the Venetian secretary Scipione Forteguerri (Hellenized as Carteromachus), and the margins are heavily annotated in his hand. It is difficult to gauge the seriousness with which the proposals are put forward: the Academy appears in this broadside to be a dining club devoted to erudite discussions *in Greek*, failure to use which will result in fines which will then be used to subsidize further banquets. The Academy appears in the preface to Sophocles (the text dated August 1502, but the

28
The opening of Genesis in Hebrew, Greek and Latin, a proof sheet from the failed project to print a *Polyglot Bible*, 1501
BN Paris, MS Grec 3064, fol 86
Reproduced by courtesy of the Bibliothèque Nationale de France

preface will be of that winter) as a discussion circle in which Musurus reports a conversation with the dedicatee Janus Lascaris – Lascaris spoke of the revival of Greek letters and the great services Aldus was performing on their behalf

The Vatican *Lex Neacademiae* appears to run together light-hearted regulation of a dining club with a plan for something much more serious and ambitious. What this was is hinted at in a number of letters to, from and between northern friends of Aldus in the first five years of the century The most definite statement comes from Johannes Cuno, the Dominican who had lived in Aldus's household and assisted at the press In December 1505 he wrote to his fellow humanist Willibald Pirckheimer (who had his own Aldines illuminated by Durer) that Aldus would soon be coming to Germany to found his New Academy under the protection of the Holy Roman Emperor Maximilian Learned men would help him instruct the youth of Germany, for whom Aldus would also print the needful books in Greek and Hebrew. If all this has a quality of academic fantasy about it, Aldus had at any rate for some years cultivated close contacts at the court of Maximilian and had printed two minor works dedicated to the emperor himself It looks as if the protracted negotiations broke down in the face of strains developing between the empire and the Venetian republic, strains which shortly issued in open war. From 1506 onwards the term 'New Academy' surfaces at irregular intervals, variously connected with a move to Naples, Milan or (most insistently) Rome. As late as 1513 separate dedications to Lucrezia Borgia, Duchess of Ferrara, and to Pope Leo X express the now forlorn hope that the ruler will at length support the creation of a learned academy, 'for which I have laboured for so many years' The pope did indeed set up a Greek college, with Janus Lascaris and Marcus Musurus and a resident Greek press – but without Aldus

These yearnings – academic in all senses – seem to have been prompted by a measure of disillusion with the hard graft and uncertain rewards of printing The Aldine press in its last ten years, from 1506 to 1515, is a very stop-go affair In January 1505 Aldus married his partner Torresani's daughter Maria in a sort of dynastic union common among printers. A year later there was a formal unification of the two partners' assets, at which time Aldus moved across the Grand Canal to take up permanent residence in the Torresani house in Campo San Paternian But no more books were printed for two years after the Virgil of December 1505, which included works of which Aldus's own preface expresses pointed disapproval 'but I was obliged to satisfy others'. The ensuing period is effectively a blank in his career, though we learn from Cuno that the two largest remaining Greek projects, Plutarch and Plato, were being discussed in 1506. What is clear is that it was an approach of the great Dutch humanist Erasmus that caused Aldus to take up presswork again

בראשית
ברא
אלהים
את
השמים ואת הארץ׃ והארץ
היתה תהו ובהו וחשך על
פני תהום ורוח אלהים
מרחפת על פני המים׃ ויאמר
אלהים יהי אור ויהי אור׃ וירא
אלהים את האור כי טוב ו
יבדל אלהים בין האור ובין
החשך׃ ויקרא אלהים לאור
יום ולחשך קרא לילה ויהי
ערב ויהי בקר יום אחד׃
ויאמר אלהים יהי רקיע בתוך
המים ויהי מבדיל בין מים
למים׃ ויעש אלהים את
הרקיע ויבדל בין המים אשר
מתחת לרקיע ובין המים א
שר מעל לרקיע ויהי כן׃ ו
יקרא אלהים לרקיע שמים
ויהי ערב ויהי בקר יום שני׃
ויאמר אלהים יקוו
המים מתחת השמים אל
מקום אחד ותראה היבשה
ויהי כן׃ ויקרא אלהים ליבשה
ארץ ולמקוה המים קרא
ימים וירא אלהים כי טוב׃ ו
יאמר אלהים תדשא הארץ
דשא עשב מזריע זרע עץ פרי
עשה פרי למינו אשר זרעו בו
על הארץ ויהי כן׃ ותוצא
הארץ דשא עשב מזריע זרע
למינהו ועץ עשה פרי אשר
זרעו בו למינהו וירא אלהים
כי טוב׃ ויהי ערב ויהי בקר
יום שלישי׃ ויאמר
אלהים יהי מארת ברקיע
השמים להבדיל בין היום
ובין הלילה והיו לאתת ו
למועדים ולימים ושנים׃ והיו
למאורת ברקיע השמים
להאיר על הארץ ויהי כן׃ ו

Ν ἀρχῇ ἐποίησεν ὁ θεὸς
τὸν οὐρανὸν, καὶ τὴν γῆν. ἡ δὲ γῆ
ἦν ἀόρατος, καὶ ἀκατα-
σκεύαστος. καὶ σκότος ἐπά-
νω τῆς ἀβύσσου. καὶ πνεῦμα θεοῦ ἐπεφέ-
ρετο ἐπάνω τοῦ ὕδατος. καὶ εἶπεν ὁ θεὸς, γενη-
θήτω φῶς. καὶ ἐγένετο φῶς. καὶ εἶδεν ὁ θεὸς τὸ
φῶς ὅτι καλόν. καὶ διεχώρισεν ὁ θεὸς ἀνὰ μέσον τοῦ φωτὸς καὶ ἀνὰ μέσον τοῦ σκότους. καὶ ἐκάλεσεν ὁ θεὸς τὸ φῶς ἡμέραν. καὶ τὸ σκότος ἐκά-
λεσε νύκτα. καὶ ἐγένετο ἑσπέρα. καὶ ἐγένετο
πρωῒ ἡμέρα μία. Καὶ εἶπεν ὁ θεὸς γενηθή-
τω στερέωμα ἐν μέσῳ τοῦ ὕδατος. καὶ ἔστω δια-
χωρίζον ἀνὰ μέσον ὕδατος καὶ ὕδατος. καὶ ἐποίησεν ὁ θεὸς τὸ στερέωμα. καὶ διεχώρισεν ὁ θεὸς ἀνὰ μέσον
τοῦ ὕδατος ὃ ἦν ὑποκάτω τοῦ στερεώματος.
καὶ ἀνὰ μέσον τοῦ ὕδατος τοῦ ἐπάνω τοῦ στερεώματος. καὶ ἐγένετο οὕτως. καὶ ἐκάλεσεν ὁ θεὸς τὸ
στερέωμα οὐρανόν. καὶ εἶδεν ὁ θεὸς ὅτι καλόν. καὶ ἐγένετο ἑσπέρα. καὶ
ἐγένετο πρωῒ ἡμέρα δευτέρα. Καὶ εἶπεν
ὁ θεὸς, συναχθήτω τὸ ὕδωρ τὸ ὑποκάτω τοῦ
οὐρανοῦ εἰς συναγωγὴν μίαν. καὶ ὀφθήτω
ἡ ξηρά. καὶ ἐγένετο οὕτως. καὶ ἐκάλεσεν ὁ θεὸς
τὴν ξηρὰν γῆν. καὶ τὰ συστήματα τῶν ὑδάτων ἐ-
κάλεσε θαλάσσας. καὶ εἶδεν ὁ θεὸς ὅτι καλόν. καὶ εἶπεν ὁ θεός. βλαστησάτω ἡ γῆ βοτάνην χόρτου σπεῖρον σπέρμα, καὶ ξύλον
κάρπιμον ποιοῦν καρπὸν κατὰ γένος. καὶ κα-
θ' ὁμοιότητα. οὗ τὸ σπέρμα αὐτοῦ ἐν αὐτῷ ἐ-
πὶ τῆς γῆς. καὶ ἐγένετο οὕτως. καὶ ἐξήνεγκεν ἡ
γῆ βοτάνην χόρτου σπεῖρον σπέρμα κατὰ
γένος, καὶ καθ' ὁμοιότητα. καὶ ξύλον κάρπιμον ποιοῦν καρπὸν, οὗ τὸ σπέρμα αὐτοῦ ἐν
αὐτῷ κατὰ γένος. καὶ εἶδεν ὁ θεὸς ὅτι καλόν. καὶ ἐγένετο ἑσπέρα. καὶ ἐγένετο πρωῒ
ἡμέρα τρίτη. Καὶ εἶπεν ὁ θεός, γενη-
θήτωσαν φωστῆρες ἐν τῷ στερεώματι τοῦ
οὐρανοῦ τοῦ διαχωρίζειν ἀνὰ μέσον τῆς ἡμέρας, καὶ ἀνὰ μέσον τῆς νυκτός. καὶ ἔστωσαν
εἰς σημεῖα, καὶ εἰς καιροὺς, καὶ εἰς ἡμέρας,
καὶ εἰς ἐνιαυτούς. καὶ ἔστωσαν εἰς φαῦσιν
ἐν τῷ στερεώματι τοῦ οὐρανοῦ, ὥστε
φαίνειν ἐπὶ τῆς γῆς. καὶ ἐγένετο οὕτως.

Nprincipio creauit
deus cælum, & ter
ram. terra autẽ erat
inanis, & uacua, &
tenebræ erant super faciem abyssi,
& spiritus domini ferebatur super
aquas. dixitq; deus fiat lux, & facta
ẽ lux. et uidit deus lucem, quod
esset bona, & diuisit lucem a tene
bris. appellauitq; lucẽ diem, & te
nebras noctem, factumq; est uespe
re & mane dies unus. Dixit
quoq; deus fiat firmamentum in
medio aquarum, & diuidat aquas
ab aquis. & fecit deus firmamẽtum
diuisitq; aquas, quæ erant sub fir
mamẽto ab iis, quæ erant super fir
mamẽtũ, & factum ẽ ita. uocauitq;
deus firmamẽtũ cælum & factum
est uespere & mane dies secundus.
Dixit uero deus, congregentur
aquæ quæ sub cælo sũt in locum
[illegible]
ẽ ita, & uocauit deus aridam ter
ram, & congregationes aquarũ ap
pellauit maria, & uidit deus q; eẽt
bonum, et ait germinet terra herbã
uirentem & facientem semen, & li
gnum pomiferum faciẽs fructum
iuxta genus suũ, cuius semen in se
metipso sit sup terram, & factum
ẽ ita. & protulit terra herbam uiren
tem, & facientem semẽ iuxta genus
suum, lignumq; faciẽs fructum,
& habens unũ quodq; sementẽ se
cũdum speciem suam. et uidit de
us q; esset bonum, & factum ẽ ue
spere & mane dies tertius. Dixit
ãt deus fiant luminaria in firmamẽ
to cæli, & diuidant diẽ, ac noctẽ,
& sint in signa, & tẽpora, & dies, &
ãnos, & luceant in firmamẽto cæli
& illuminent terrã, et factũ est ita.

29
Aldus Manutius, *Introductio utilissima hebraice discere cupientibus*, about 1500
Aldus's introduction to the Hebrew language survives as a separate publication only in this miniature volume, printed in red and black
Original page-size 95×66 mm
Rylands 11278, fols 14v and 16r (letter of Aldus)
Reproduced by courtesy of The John Rylands University Library, University of Manchester

Erasmus had been a year in Italy when he felt the need of some book to present to potential patrons at Rome, and asked Aldus if he would undertake a reprint of his Euripidean translations The previous edition, he was careful to explain, had sold well in Paris the year before, and he would be glad to have a printer of Aldus's stature – a sort of immortality in itself – and the fine and careful printing for which the press was renowned The upshot of this was the issue of Euripides at the end of 1507 More importantly, it brought Erasmus to stay by Aldus's invitation at the printing establishment in San Paternian for some eight months in 1508

This sojourn produced late in Erasmus's life, after he had fallen out with Alberto Pio, a sour sketch of the miserable fare provided in the Torresani household in the colloquy *Opulentia sordida* ('The Rich Miser') But it also produced a famous book, the Aldine *Adagia*, completely reworked and greatly expanded from the slim first edition that Erasmus had had printed in Paris in 1500. The *Adagia* as it appeared in September 1508 is a large collection of classical proverbs and maxims with extensive and enlightening commentary by Erasmus The passages of comment sometimes amount to little tracts of mingled erudition, observation and (increasingly in later editions) personal reminiscence and polemic In the long explication of *Festina lente* ('hasten slowly'), for example, Erasmus makes use of an ancient coin that Bembo had given Aldus to tease out the suggestive design of the dolphin and anchor, this provides the occasion for the remark that thanks to Aldus, the image is known and loved wherever good learning is cherished, and for a prolonged puff of the Aldine programme in general – Hebrew is still mentioned, even a proposal to print in Syriac. The author made generous acknowledgement of the unfailing help of the members of the Aldine 'Academy' in supplying out of the way sources, often Greek and from their own manuscripts.

We have a vivid later picture from Erasmus of his work at this time: he would sit in one corner of the printing office actually writing the *Adagia*, passing the completed sheets to the compositor for immediate setting up, while in another corner sat Aldus reading through the proofs, waving aside interruptions with the single word *studeo* ('I'm working') Of such chaos was a great book born The *Adagia*, in this edition thoroughly indexed and prefaced by a complimentary letter of Aldus, rapidly became indispensable to studious readers and writers as a window on the ancient world, affording as it did a virtual anthology of classical literature It was the book that first brought Erasmus a European reputation He also took a minor role at this time, alongside the editor Demetrius Ducas, in putting together the long-planned Plutarch, which finally appeared in March 1509 (Fig 27)

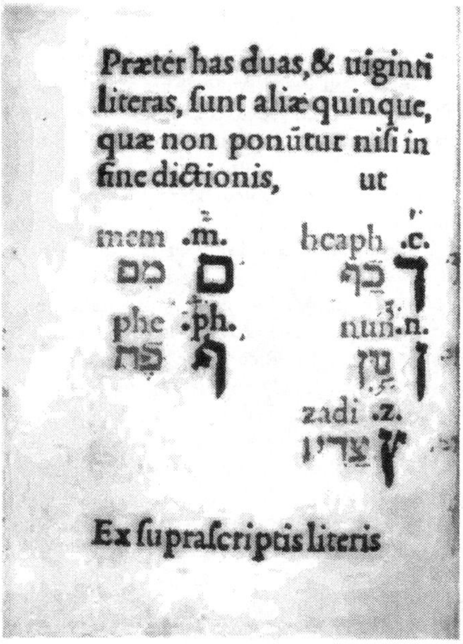

Præter has duas,& uiginti
literas, sunt aliæ quinque,
quæ non ponũtur nisi in
fine dictionis, ut

mem .m. heaph .c.
מם ם כף ך
phe .ph. nun .n.
פה ף נון ן
zadi .z.
צדין ץ

Ex suprascriptis literis

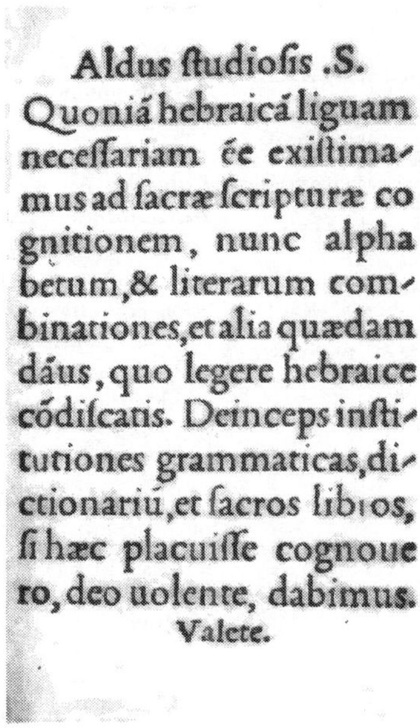

Aldus studiosis .S.
Quoniã hebraicã liguam
necessariam ẽe existima-
mus ad sacræ scripturæ co
gnitionem, nunc alpha
betum,& literarum com-
binationes,et alia quædam
dãus, quo legere hebraice
cõdiscatis. Deinceps insti-
tutiones grammaticas,di-
ctionariũ,et sacros libros,
si hæc placuisse cognoue
ro, deo uolente, dabimus.
Valete.

THE LAST YEARS

The second volume of the Greek rhetoricians issued in May 1509 was to prove the last major production of the Aldine press for three years or more. The upheavals which the intervention of French and imperial troops had brought to Italy in the first decade of the sixteenth century were now for the first time touching Venice directly. The League of Cambrai was an anti-Venetian alliance led by the Pope Julius II, which made it unsafe for Aldus – still, as ever, a Roman citizen – to remain in Venice. Until June 1512 he was absent from the city, taking his family off to live in Ferrara and seeking to protect his landed property in the Venetian *terra firma*, now in the process of dismemberment by the League. In Ferrara in August 1511 he made the second of his wills to survive,

30
The 'Regulations of the New Academy', about 1501 A single sheet composed by Scipione Forteguerri setting out the organization of the dining club and learned society called the *Neacademia* Città del Vaticano, BAV, Stamp Barb AAA IV 13
Reproduced by courtesy of the Biblioteca Apostolica Vaticana

still voicing there the hope that he might found the 'Academy' It was not until the end of 1512 that printing resumed at Venice, then to undergo a surprising, but for Aldus short-lived, efflorescence in the two years that remained to him His return to printing is credited to the persuasion of Venetian friends, and in particular Andrea Navagero, later the Librarian of the Biblioteca Marciana, who became in these last years the main editor of the Aldine Latin books, beside Musurus's work on the Greek texts

Against a dark background of almost unbroken Venetian disasters, a rather desperate optimism breaks out afresh in the preface of the octavo Pindar of January 1513, dedicated to Navagero. Venice was again seen, as Musurus had seen it in the 1498 Aristophanes, as the new Athens. Learned books of all sorts – Greek, Latin and the long-heralded Hebrew – were to be printed, with this Pindar 'ex Academia nostra' first in line Aldus puts on record his sense of the sacrifices involved in twenty years of labour at the printing press, 'but I have resolved never to shrink from benefiting mankind' It seems to have been a genuine mission with him.

A sense of a new beginning may also have come with the election of Pope Leo X, son of Lorenzo de' Medici, in March 1513. This at any rate is the tenor of Aldus's preface to the pope which accompanied the Greek *editio princeps* of Plato: just as the Wars of Italy had followed on the death of Lorenzo, so the election of Leo may bring them to a close

The Plato in two large folio volumes was the last great undertaking of the first Aldine press, a work promised already in 1497 and certainly worked on at least from 1506, now finally presented to the world in September 1513 The preface is unusually elaborate for Aldus, who here shows the fierce pride he took in his accomplishments He reports the views of friends (too kind, he says), that he had single-handedly done more to help literature than anyone for centuries But although his only ambition had been to provide students with books 'as correct and beautiful as they could be', never yet had he been satisfied with any edition, and he would gladly pay a gold ducat for every mistake he had since noticed The appeal for papal support of the Aldine Academy which follows fell, as we have seen, on deaf ears. But some good came of Aldus's praise of his editor, Marcus Musurus, by now professor of Greek at Venice. The elegy with which Musurus introduced the text is a moving lament for the destruction of the Greek homeland and an appeal for support of Hellenic studies it has been called the finest Greek poem of the Renaissance In the event Leo selected Musurus to head his Greek college in Rome after Aldus's death. The text of Plato shows signs of having drawn upon the manuscripts of Cardinal Bessarion, a leading light of fifteenth-century Platonism (Aldus had republished his *In calumniatorem Platonis* in 1503) It is unclear whether these were directly

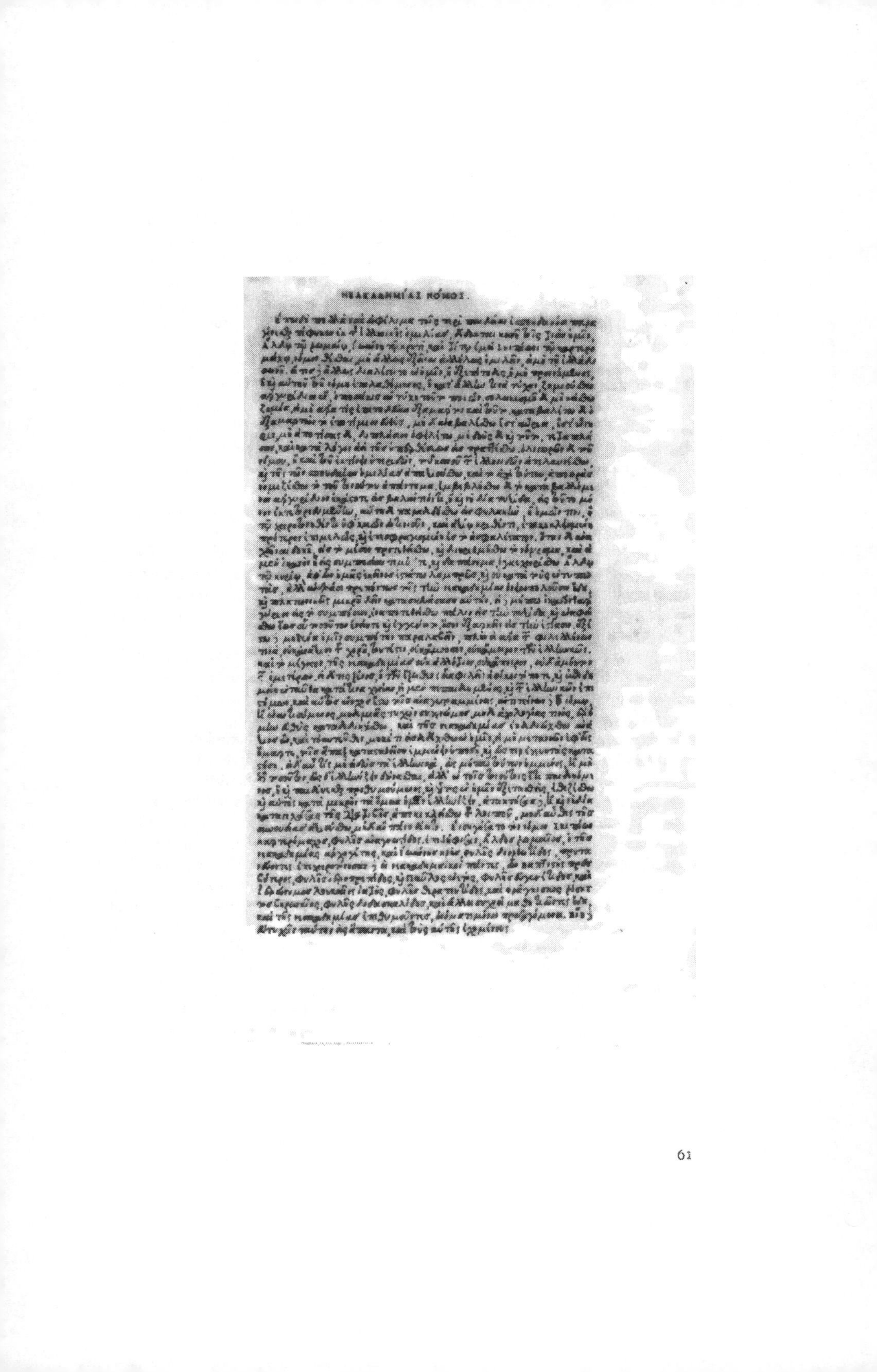

[illegible]

accessible in Venice even in 1513, and the Aldine text may rest instead on copies taken before the long hibernation of the cardinal's legacy to Venice

Plato was far from the only Greek text being put to the press in this period, but it was the largest and most important The Attic orators, apart from the already published Demosthenes, appeared in Greek in two volumes in April and May of 1513. The rest were decidedly a minority taste. The Byzantine lexica of Suidas and Hesychius, and the curious mélange of ancient social customs preserved in the *Deipnosophistae* of Athenaeus, all of them edited with great skill by Musurus, were for scholars only The Greek folios were once more buoyed up by a steady stream of quarto reprints of standard Latin authors, grammars in Greek and Latin, and octavo classics in Latin and Italian. These now included a larger element of modern poets Jacopo Sannazaro's *Arcadia*, a popular exercise in vernacular pastoral, and the Latin poems of Aldus's friends Gian Gioviano Pontano (reprinted from the edition of 1505) and the Strozzi of Ferrara (the younger of whom had been Aldus's pupil) All in all this last period was as busy for Aldus as any since the beginning of the century The unusually revealing preface to the rhetorical works of Cicero (March 1514) makes public a notice he had caused to be set up over the door of his room to deter the crowds of would-be authors and the idle curious who otherwise interrupted his labours 'Whoever you are, state your business as briefly as possible and be gone, unless you are willing to shoulder his burdens, as Hercules did for weary Atlas '

Weariness with his long task had set in, compounded by the distress – moral and no doubt economic – brought by the continuing wars that vexed Italy. Aldus had now been printing, with intermissions, for twenty years, a considerable stretch for an early printer, and he was in his seventh decade, very much an old man by Renaissance standards. From mid-1514 his health began to fail, in January 1515 he made his last will, and on 6 February of that year he died His last book, though by no means the last he planned, was a Lucretius, newly edited by Navagero and dedicated like his very first publications in philosophy to Alberto Pio And it was to Pio and to his fragile principality of Carpi that his last thoughts turned His will instructs that he is to be buried there, in a place that the prince shall decide Before removal to Carpi (if it ever took place), his body lay in ceremony in the parish church of San Paternian, surrounded by his books

Aldus's work passed to others, to his sons and to his father-in-law Torresani, who remained surprisingly faithful to the spirit of the founder What was left were the hundred and twenty or so editions that his fame is founded upon Those editions rest in turn upon the vision which informs everything he printed a humanist conviction that good letters lead, under God's guidance, to good men, and that the best letters were in Greek By the time of his death Aldus had transformed the face of learning in Europe: only Aeschylus of the major Greek

authors remained to be printed, an achievement of the Aldine press in 1518. Aldus was not himself an author in any active sense – he never published more than the grammar which Erasmus said he wrote five times over. His editions can often be faulted for their presswork and proof-reading, and views differ on the merits of the types he employed. The texts he put out were sometimes poorly edited, compiled in haste and under pressure. But when the protagonist of Thomas More's *Utopia* (1516) wants to teach the Utopians how to print, it is naturally the Greek books of Aldus that he shows them, symbols of the best that European literature and technology could offer. Contemporaries like More and Erasmus understood his greatness in securing the foundations and diffusion of classical studies, and so, five hundred years on, can we.

CPSIA information can be obtained
at www.ICGtesting.com
Printed in the USA
BVHW091731181118
533417BV00003B/197/P

9 781376 144277